KU-028-453

THE

GRAND DESIGN

CRAFTSMANSHIP IN INTERIOR DECORATION

THE GRAND DESIGN

CRAFTSMANSHIP IN INTERIOR DECORATION

Marie Clayton

with an Introduction by Beverly Russell

Published in 1992 by Hazar Publishing Ltd
147 Chiswick Road London W4 2DT
in association with Editions Hazar Paris

A catalogue record for this title is available from the British Library

ISBN - 1-874371-00-8

Acknowledgement

Quotations in the introduction attributed to H.R.H. The Prince of Wales are reproduced from Charles Jencks, The Prince, The Architects and the New Wave Monarchy, published by Academy Editions.

Introduced by Beverly Russell

Text by Marie Clayton

Designed by John Spedding Design Consultants

Typeset/Filmset by BBB Design London

Printed and bound by Milanostampa S.p.A. Italy

CONTENTS

EXIT

INTRODUCTION

The new appreciation for arts and crafts

Toward the end of the 19th Century and at the beginning of the 20th Century, handcrafts were practised in partnership with architecture. There was hardly an architect who did not involve a team of artisans to work on all aspects of a building, from the exterior stonework to the interior marble fireplaces, carved wood staircases, intricate inlaid marquetry furniture, chandeliers, wrought-iron work and stained glass windows. This was true all over Europe and in the United States. Indeed the most prominent messengers of this particular school, Charles Rennie Mackintosh, Frank Lloyd Wright and Josef Hoffmann frequently crossed national boundaries to discuss the integration of arts and architecture. Their interactions went far beyond just the exchange of ideas, to the broader and deeper philosophy of the use of crafts. By their very nature, crafts represent a unity of hand and spirit, the manifestation of the difference that a single person can make to a whole entity. The use of crafts, therefore, has a higher purpose; to give citizens, who can readily identify with this artisan activity, a sense of connection with aesthetics.

Sadly, during the course of the 20th Century as the world has been engulfed in a technological "explosion", the value of the handcrafted process has been diminished. Men who had earned an honest living in the craftshop or atelier, turned to more mechanized factory jobs. Women, who in Victorian times had spent long hours sewing, knitting, crocheting, embroidering or quilting, have been caught up in a social evolution of such power and momentum that the old-fashioned domestic pursuits have been pushed to the background. As the century comes to a close, however, it is clear that the machine age and technology are not all that they were cracked up to be. The notion that industrialization would make a better and improved world for everybody has not altogether proved to be a reality. Mass production has produced a society so dedicated to consumption that the pollution of earth, air and waters has reached the point where not only the globe but the human species has become endangered.

In the realm of architecture and design, for most of this century, the prevailing dominance of Modernism drastically restricted the use of handcrafts. The underlying principle behind the Modern school of design (also known as the International Style because of its transnational application) grew from a valid belief that a society moving toward social equality and opportunity for all called for a uniformity of geometry. Expressions of economy and spareness signalled a departure from the social hierarchies. Decorative roof-lines, symbolizing crowns and castles, were rejected in favour of the flat-topped, unadorned boxes that spread with amazing alacrity throughout the globe. Unfortunately the simplicity of this design form led to a repetitive formula that produced millions of undistinguished concrete-and-glass structures. Not only were these buildings - by virtue of their ever-increasing numbers - boring to look at, but it was hard to tell the difference between a school, an office, a bank, a hotel or a hospital. Rigid similarity destroyed idiosyncratic characteristics. Regional and neighborhood familiarity were blithely bulldozed away in the name of this "good" design for the "new" era. With them went all respect for decorative arts and crafts, which simply didn't exist during the Modernist period because architects didn't want to use them.

Today we are seeing the world with new eyes. There is now a popular reaction to an intellectual movement that obliterated history and memories, whether in Birmingham, England, Chicago, Illinois, Glasgow, Scotland, or The Hague in the Netherlands. The consensus is overwhelmingly for a reconsideration of the past and an appreciation of the value of building and interior decoration that embodies the continuum of life. While technology cannot be wholeheartedly abandoned, it is not a valid metaphor for human hopes and aspirations. The past cannot be wiped out, it must be confronted. For this reason, the desire to preserve and restore old landmarks and neighborhoods is causing an amazing change in the context of building and design today. Architecture schools have been forced to open up departments specializing in historical restoration, for example. There has been an extraordinary rise in the influence of the discipline of interior design - mostly because the architecture schools abandoned their interior design education at the door step of a building, concentrating on mass, facade and construction, with little consideration of the manipulation and comfort of the space within. Yet the idea of the universal interior space, with wall-less zones and flexible furniture, was quickly rejected by the users of Le Corbusier's famous low-cost housing units in France. Once installed in these units, people instantly expressed their preferences for good old-fashioned rooms, and the psychological benefits of privacy and coziness, by putting up divisions and creating "nests" and "niches".

The depiction of technology as a spiritual force, and thus the guiding impetus of a design movement, is no longer plausible. It follows that architects and designers are faced with the challenge of discovering new and appropriate imagery for our society. This is the message articulated by Prince Charles, who has been so roundly criticized by certain members of the architectural profession but so loudly applauded by ordinary citizens on both sides of the Atlantic. There is still resistance in the profession to his point of view, but there are more than a few signs that the tide is turning. The so-called Post-Modernist movement, which began in the early 1970's in the United States, led by Michael Graves, Charles Moore, Robert A.M. Stern and Robert Venturi, was the beginning of the reversal.

It was critic Charles Jencks who coined the term Post-Modernist to encompass trends which went counter to orthodox Modernism. Three broad principles were defined: ornamentalism, contextualism and allusionism. With these principles came the understanding that the glass or concrete box, for all its elegant simplicity and political connotation, was not the ideal universal structure. It was unornamented, it never fitted into its context, and it didn't allude to anything. To the Post-Modernists variety, history and decoration were to be applauded, not deplored. A seminal book published in 1977, "Body, Memory and Architecture", co-authored by Charles Moore with his Yale University friend and colleague Kent Bloomer, codified the reasons for the counter-cultural ideology. The Bloomer and Moore hypothesis introduced two key words: haptic and syncretic. "Haptic" expresses a system by which the sense of touch is reconsidered to include the entire body. "Syncretic" implies a collage-like layering of decoration that, while full of complexity and tradition, remains accessible to ordinary people. The purpose of design should not be to produce an object, they argued, but to create a feeling derived from the object - whether it is a house, with its rooms having an air of happy domesticity, or a chair, with its aspects of physical comfort and support. With this manifesto the wheel turned full circle, back to a renewed appreciation for

Introduction

handcraftsmanship, opening the door to a reassimilation of the stained glass, stenciling, mural painting, metalwork and numerous other crafts-orientated skills that had been fundamental to architecture previously. In 1982 two prominent design professionals, Patricia Conway and Robert Jensen, followed up with a book called "Ornamentalism", showing examples of the use of crafts in full swing. They recorded that collecting crafts had become an aesthetic passion, due to the richness of ornament they offered and the heightened appreciation for past decorative styles.

While architects were busy putting an intellectual handle to the decorative arts renaissance, and a new avant garde group of designers were reinvestigating classical Beaux Arts principles (the idea, for example, that a building should have a "bottom", a "middle" and a "top"), by the 1980's it became very clear that the artisans of the world were alive and well. They began taking responsibility for their own recognition and acceptance by a public eager to get their hands on one-of-a-kind, personal objects, with an individual, non-mass-produced stamp. Crafts Fairs suddenly flourished and statistics were vigorously gathered about the revival. In the United States, by the 1990's, studies showed that 92 per cent of Americans acknowledged that the arts were important to the quality of life in their own community, and half a million professional craftspeople were busy contributing to a two-and-a-half billion dollar annual industry. A rapid increase in the number of college courses and workshops provided teaching posts for craftspeople, who were now considered part of the establishment workforce and not a "flaky" group on the fringe of the mainstream. In Great Britain crafts boomed, with the annual Chelsea Crafts Fair in 1991 raking in almost one million pounds of revenue in a recessionary year, actually posting a profit over the preceding Fair of 1990.

The overwhelmingly positive reception to handcraftsmanship has been identified with two important attributes. Firstly, ornamentalism expresses the aspirations of society; secondly, handcrafted decoration provides a reference point of scale within a space to which the human body can relate. Chair rails and floor patterns, stenciling and mural decoration can bring the four walls of an interior space into connection with the eye and make relationships to the human figure, thus giving a person a sense of belonging and a feeling of being comfortable within the space. Moreover, by judiciously setting standards, the individual craftsperson is able to make a political statement that resonates with the public. For example, the British furniture maker John Makepeace firmly believes that craftspeople and artists can alter the perceptions of consumer culture by taking responsibility for the effects their creations have on the environment. Makepeace tries to avoid consumption of rare and imported woods for the creation of furniture and utilitarian objects. Not only does that practice deplete natural resources in the countries where these woods are forested, he points out, but shipping materials halfway round the world is an added expense and expenditure of our resources of oil, which is not necessary.

If the 1990's can be described by one attitude above any other, it is a quest for quality. Across a wide spectrum of industries, quality items and services are in great demand. People are "value conscious". This trend, according to futurist Roger Seilbert, will help to promote the increasing development of handcraftsmanship. The same people, in fact, who search for low-cost value, will also search for high-priced, high-quality items with which to enhance their lives at home. There is a recognizable shift in taste - toward a consideration of the intrinsic "essence" of an object.

The Grand Design records this shift. It is a celebration of what Prince Charles has called the "pleasure and delight of artists and craftsmen returning to architecture after their long exile." It is indeed exhilarating to know that all over Europe craftshops and ateliers are actually flourishing - producing the kind of exquisite custom work seen in the numerous examples on the following pages.

In a London atelier, for example, you will find two or three craftswomen screen-printing sumptuous handwoven silks and chiffons. When this process is complete, the artists will go over certain floral details with a stencil and a stipple brush. They may further adorn the fabric with bead work, sequins, diamanté, or gold thread embroidery. Aside from creating fabrics for well-known fashion designers, such as Thea Porter and Bill Gibb, the atelier supplies a very special clientele with fabrics and companion wallpapers for their residences. A lady from New Zealand, for example, will order 40 metres of fabric for two big windows of her farmhouse near Toulouse. A client from Manhattan will demand custom designs for all the window treatments for two townhouses that are being made into one very glamorous residence. A member of a royal family prefers an Italian silk for a bedroom, printed with waterlilies, and orders the design to be handwoven into matching carpet. To have a special fabric like this is like owning a painting. It reflects the work of a very special artist, it has qualities that cannot be described easily in words. There is an element which transcends beauty and moves into the realm of the metaphysical, because the work embodies the spirit and presence of a person who loves, cares and attends to her craft.

In a Paris atelier, a team of artisans is busy producing marble, glass or ceramic mosaics to be installed in swimming pools, in water fountains, on floors or on walls as murals. It is breathtaking to see individual chips of marble struck off from the large stone with a hand tool - exactly as it was done in Greek and Roman times. The business is growing rapidly as people realize they want something as a contrast in their lives to the constant repetition of objects from the machine age. Thankfully there are still mosaic workers who are entering the craft, to be able to restore and recreate the ancient patterns that have been used down the centuries. Equally well, however, they can follow the design of a fine artist to produce any modern abstract or figurative scene that may be commissioned by a client.

Stained glass, which was so popular in Victorian days and so highly appreciated when designed by such important artists as Louis Comfort Tiffany and René Lalique, in recent decades has been relegated to ecclesiastical use only. Fortunately this craft, with its 800-year-old history of architectural enrichment, is receiving renewed appreciation today. At a stained glass studio in London the workshop is alive with activity. The designs are incredibly varied and may end up in such diverse places as Sleeping Beauty's Castle at Euro-Disney, a London hotel, or a sheik's palace in the Middle East. Terence Conran's Michelin House in Fulham Road is all the more striking for its three Michelin windows that were supplied to replace the original glass which was removed during World War II. In residential installations, stained glass enriches windows, skylights, domes and doors. In these days of sensitivity to the comfort of air conditioning, if solar heat penetration is considered a hazard, the skylight or dome can be actually hidden under the architectural "skin" and backlit to give the same effect as daylight.

What is particularly exhilarating about the crafts revival is that it is bringing new techniques into the crafts vocabulary. With backgrounds in painting, sculpture and design, many recent art school graduates are setting up their shops and offering a wide range of fantasy finishes - or paint techniques for interiors, furniture and objects. The decorative painter can work in the

Introduction

traditional style of the past, which goes all the way back to cave painting in charcoal and blood, embellishing walls with figurative or decorative scenes, or enhancing wood panelling, or classical interior design detailing. Techniques include ragging, sponging, stippling and dragging. They can be employed to simulate the appearance of marble, wood, precious stones, metal, or more commonplace surfaces such as canvas, fabrics and plaster. Today decorative artists also go beyond faithfully copying, making colour and compositional adjustments to suit specific clients or decorative requirements. The idea that successful results do not necessarily depend on the authentic replication of any particular subject or phenomena is where the element of fantasy comes in, opening up unlimited opportunities for unusual effects and environments.

Perhaps most important in this reassessment of interior decoration and the value of craftsmanship relates to the longevity of the work. It is a false claim that the products of craftspeople are "luxuries", because they often have a far longer life than a ready-made decorative element - a wall mural will survive longer than a wallpaper, for example. A handpainted fabric or a handcrafted piece of furniture - even a hand decorated vase or pot - tends to be loved and used longer by the owner simply because it has the cachet of its individual maker. Thus handcrafts help to break the insidious cycle of obsolescence, one of the current major global plagues. They also champion individualism and make a statement against technocracy, thereby fulfilling a vital need in an era of doubt and insecurity. They help to restore hope, in Prince Charles' words, "by providing a vision and a source of inspiration".

Beverly Russell

Beverly Russell

1

HALLS & RECEPTION AREAS

HALLS & RECEPTION AREAS

The entrance hall is the threshold of the building, its main practical function is as a convenient central space from which to move easily to other areas. There is a danger of it becoming a busy crossroads and losing its essential atmosphere of welcome and peace – an introduction to the building and a comfortable place in which to wait.

The reception area introduces visitors from outside into more intimate and private areas and it is generally the first internal area of a building that will be seen. As a semi-public space, where most people will not spend much time, it offers the opportunity for a strong design statement.

The attention of the visitor can be caught with a central focus point, by the creation of interesting shapes in the architecture of the space, or by using dramatic design effects which may be inappropriate elsewhere.

LEFT *A strong floor pattern is a dramatic design statement, echoing the shape of the area and also leading the eye towards other areas of the building.*

BELOW *The reception area deliberately scaled much larger than the human figure is imposing and creates an overall feeling of grandeur.*

The furniture in large scale formal reception areas can be used to define a slightly more intimate space for waiting in. Here the style of the furniture is deliberately very simple so it does not detract from the marble floor patterns and complex column detailing.

RIGHT *A sense of grandeur can be achieved, even in a fairly modest floor area, by cutting away the floor between two levels and creating a double height space. This also adds an interesting feature to the area above.*

HALLS & RECEPTION AREAS
Featuring Shapes

RIGHT *Seating areas in a large open area are given a feeling of intimacy by the use of individual table lamps to light the immediate area. Carefully placed mini-spotlights highlight the decorative stepped edge to the balcony and throw dramatic shapes on plain painted walls.*

BERKELEY

chandelier
gypsum
mirror
gypsum cornice
lacquered timber doors
sandstone + marble panels.
Decorative timber lacquered screen with stained glass panels.

Defining Areas

LEFT *The detailing of the door panels echoes the shapes in the stair balusters.*

OPPOSITE INSET *Alternative sketch scheme for the same area.*

BELOW *Looking up through the centre of the staircase to the dome with its central chandelier. The dome adds a sudden sense of drama and scale to a relatively small and intimate area.*

BOTTOM *The sweep of the staircase defines the contours of the area, creating one space for seating and another for circulation.*

OPPOSITE *The bold floor pattern and repeating pattern of the columns break up the length of a corridor. The dark colour of the door echoes the lines in the floor and creates an instant focal point.*

LEFT *Here the floor pattern leads the eye in stages towards the doors of one of the major rooms*

BELOW LEFT *The strong geometric shape of the main entrance doors contrasts in style with the rest of the area, making them a major feature in the entrance hall.*

BELOW *The hand made carpet is a splash of colour on the plain marble floor, drawing the eye towards the main doors.*

LEFT *Commercial areas offer their own problems, the volume of traffic means that finishes must be simple to maintain and hard wearing. The use of colour and geometric shapes in this shopping centre adds some interest to what would otherwise be a rather bland area.*

BELOW *The bright coloured framing and bold shape of the entrance clearly signposts the way in.*

BOTTOM *The glazed pyramid above the escalators allows natural light to flood into the area.*

OPPOSITE *Using the full height of the building in this hotel reception area again makes a relatively small floor area seem much grander in scale. It is important to keep some sort of proportion between the floor area and the ceiling height, or the space will seem uncomfortable. Here the full height central area gradually steps down to a more human scale height at each side.*

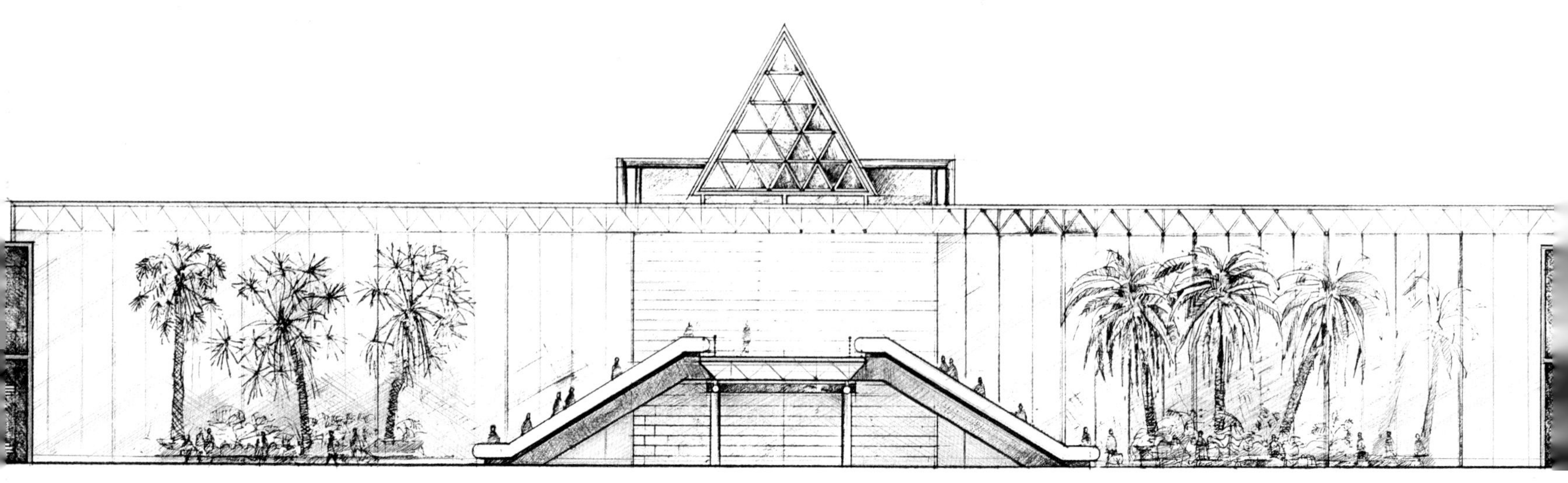

RECEPTION

HALLS & RECEPTION AREAS
Commercial and Functional

LEFT *Sketch scheme for the reception area in an international hotel. The reception must appear welcoming and comfortable, as well as setting a style for the rest of the building. Finishes and strong detailing are important.*

BELOW *The bold carpet design delineates the circulation area, essential seating is tucked into the alcoves formed by the columns to keep the central floor space open and uncluttered.*

BOTTOM *Seating arranged in intimate groups to make those waiting feel more comfortable in a very formal area.*

LIVING ROOMS

The living room is often both a formal area for entertaining guests and an informal area to relax in. It may include different areas for entertaining, for studying, for playing, for relaxing.

Formal living rooms in the grand style are in many cases principally for entertaining, so a classical design can be very appropriate. Although the furniture can still be very comfortable to sit on, it is laid out in formal groups and there may be quite large areas of open space in the room. In a more informal living room the furniture layout is much more unstructured and is designed to create an intimate atmosphere and a comfortable area to relax in.

A welcoming atmosphere is as important as a sense of style in the living room - these are rooms to spend time in, so attention to detail is vitally important. Design features must not detract from the comfort of the room, or make it difficult to use on a day to day basis.

OPPOSITE *Warm colours and the careful use of pattern give this room its welcoming atmosphere.*

BELOW *Modern deeply upholstered sofas look comfortable and invite relaxation, while the choice of colours and fabrics adds to the informal effect.*

LEFT *A classical living room with the furniture arranged in formal groups to match the style of the room.*

BELOW *A large room like this can take bold detailing and stronger colours.*

gypsum
over panel
with painted
finish.
coloured glass

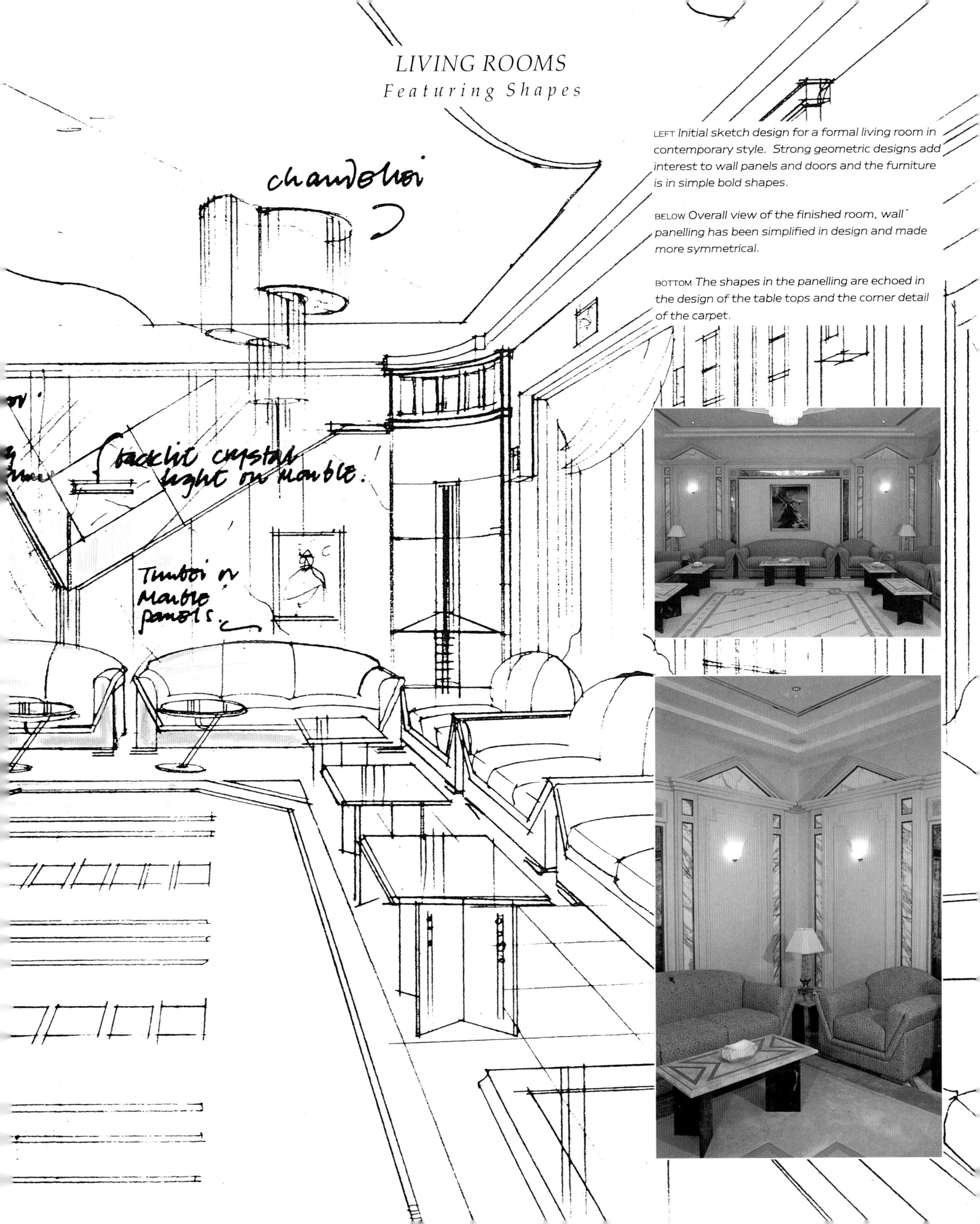

LIVING ROOMS

Featuring Shapes

LEFT *Initial sketch design for a formal living room in contemporary style. Strong geometric designs add interest to wall panels and doors and the furniture is in simple bold shapes.*

BELOW *Overall view of the finished room, wall panelling has been simplified in design and made more symmetrical.*

BOTTOM *The shapes in the panelling are echoed in the design of the table tops and the corner detail of the carpet.*

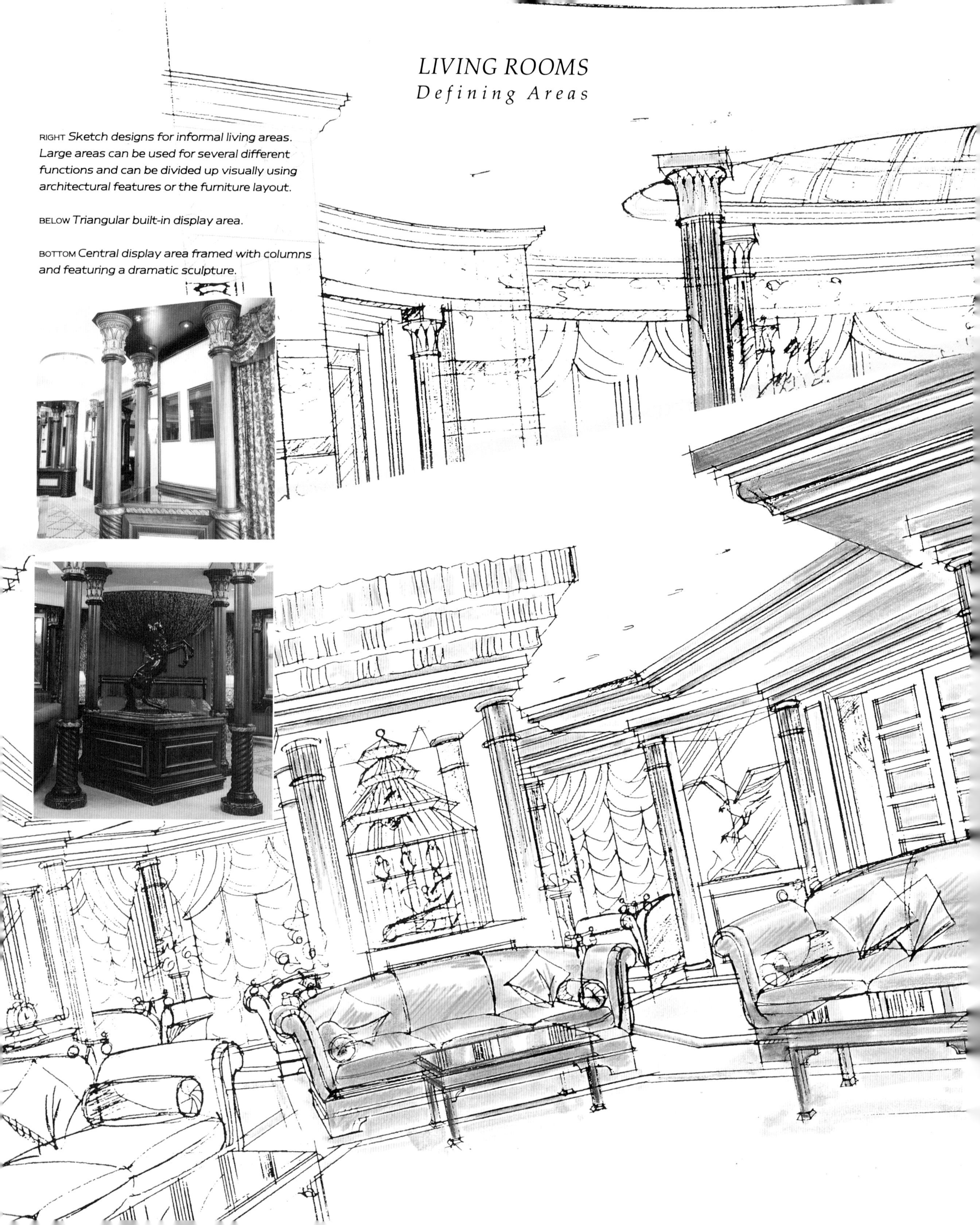

RIGHT *Sketch designs for informal living areas. Large areas can be used for several different functions and can be divided up visually using architectural features or the furniture layout.*

BELOW *Triangular built-in display area.*

BOTTOM *Central display area framed with columns and featuring a dramatic sculpture.*

BELOW *Steps down into a seating area immediately separate it from the rest of the room.*

BOTTOM *Unit seating used to define an informal area for relaxing within a more formal and classical style room.*

RIGHT *Strong bright colours are a major feature in this small living room, with several co-ordinating fabrics in blue and yellow used for curtains and seating. The walls are done in a simple stippled paint finish, using colours picked up from the fabrics.*

BELOW *Detail of the carpet design. The carpet has been specially made to match the colours in the room.*

OPPOSITE TOP *A concentration of pattern and colour in the small study seating area off the main living room draws the eye to that end of the room.*

OPPOSITE BOTTOM *Cupboards and bookcases in a special paint finish, to match the general colour scheme.*

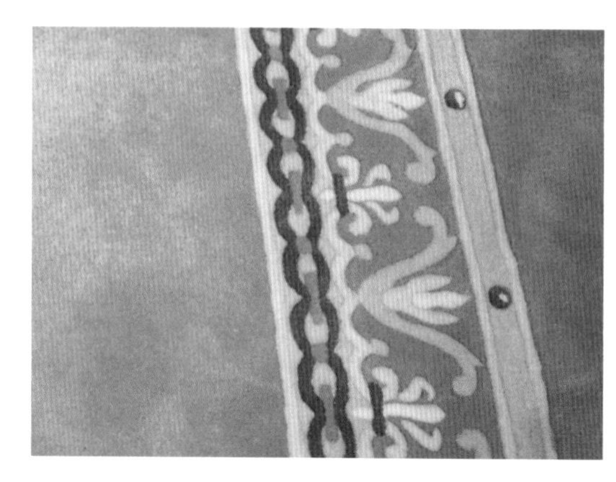

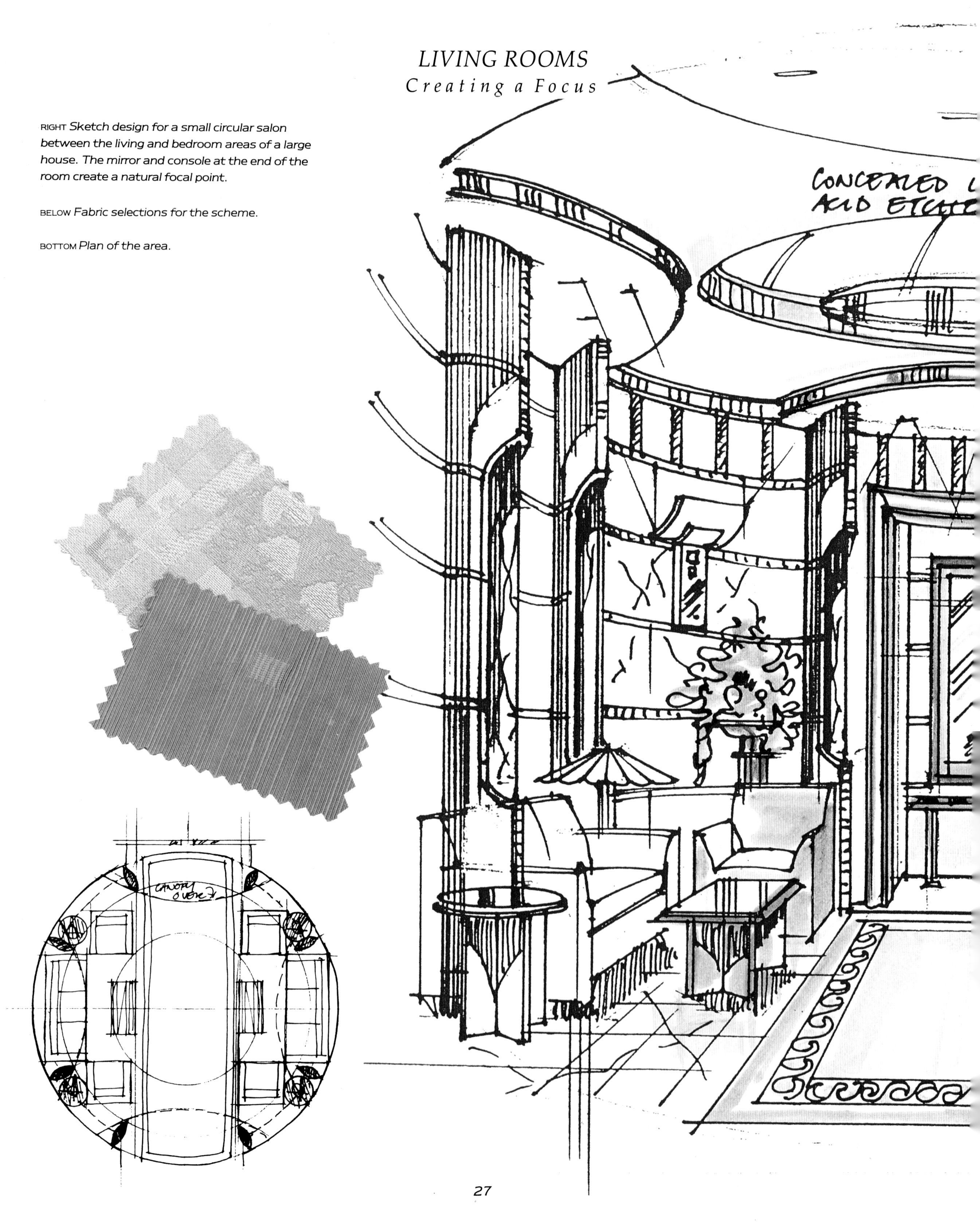

RIGHT *Sketch design for a small circular salon between the living and bedroom areas of a large house. The mirror and console at the end of the room create a natural focal point.*

BELOW *Fabric selections for the scheme.*

BOTTOM *Plan of the area.*

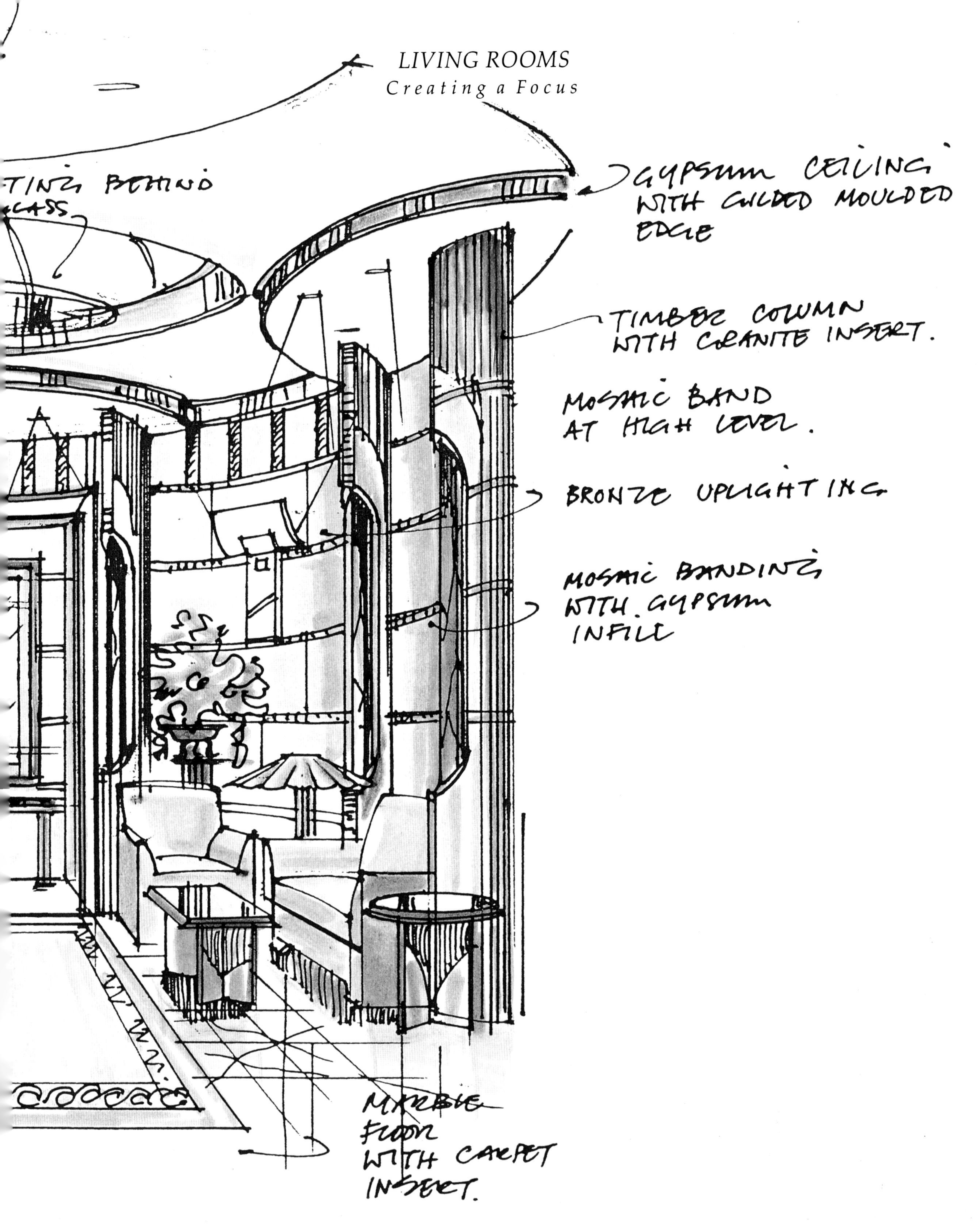
GYPSUM CEILING WITH GILDED MOULDED EDGE
TIMBER COLUMN WITH GRANITE INSERT.
MOSAIC BAND AT HIGH LEVEL.
BRONZE UPLIGHTING
MOSAIC BANDING WITH GYPSUM INFILL
MARBLE FLOOR WITH CARPET INSERT.

LIVING ROOMS
Attention to Details

OPPOSITE *Specially designed carpets and fabrics can add a touch of individuality to a room and can tie a scheme together.*

LEFT *The fabric was designed with a knot motif and a geometric border, the design was then adapted at a much larger scale for the carpet.*

BELOW *Sample boards showing the furniture, specially finished to match the general colour scheme, and the initial fabric design with the standard fabrics also used in the same room. At the bottom is a detail of the carpet border.*

DINING ROOMS

The more casual modern lifestyle has often threatened the existence of the separate dining room - particularly in smaller houses - but over the last few years they have been gaining in popularity again. As a room that is normally only in use during set times of the day, the dining room can provide an opportunity for quite dramatic design effects.

Large formal dining rooms have their own special problems. Tables must be laid out with sufficient space around them to allow circulation for the service of food, central service points must be carefully planned, while the dining room must still retain a pleasant social atmosphere. Dining rooms in the grand style should have a sense of occasion, while still being comfortable places in which to eat.

When creating a dining area in a large living room there are many ways to visually indicate the different function of the area, either by changing the floorcovering or by using architectural features.

OPPOSITE *Richly decorated columns and cornice and the use of mirrors and gold highlighting give an opulent feel to this classical dining room.*

BELOW *Large dining rooms have a sense of occasion.*

DINING ROOMS
The Grandeur of Scale

OPPOSITE *Dining rooms in the grand style should still retain a social atmosphere and be comfortable places in which to eat. The walls of this room are richly panelled in three different coloured marbles*

RIGHT *The main entrance doors are just under three metres high, but the layers of decorative banding and the shape of the arch above make them appear visually in scale with the rest of the room.*

BOTTOM *A row of six metre high arched windows is a strong feature along one wall and the arch shape is echoed in the panelling in the rest of the room.*

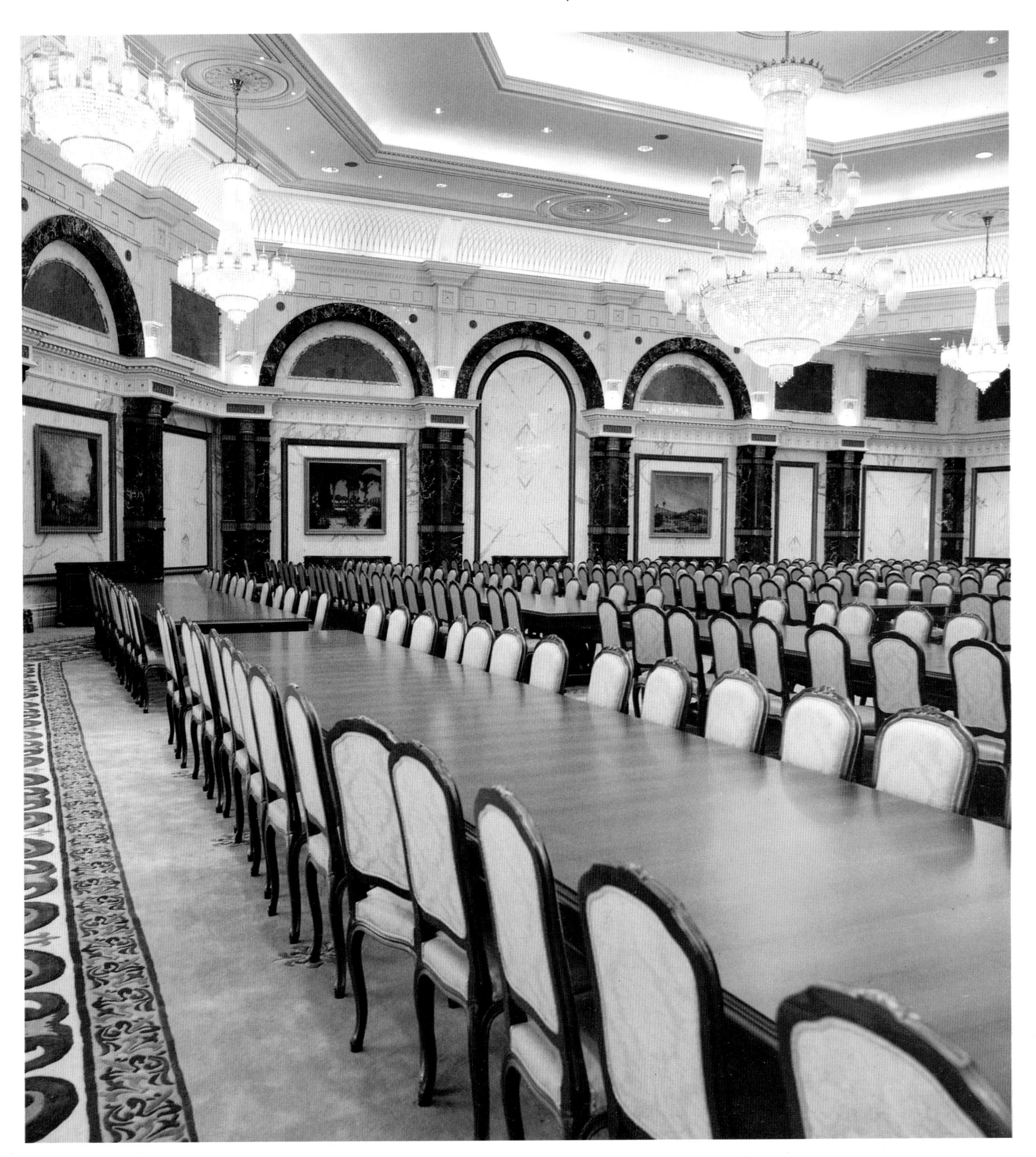

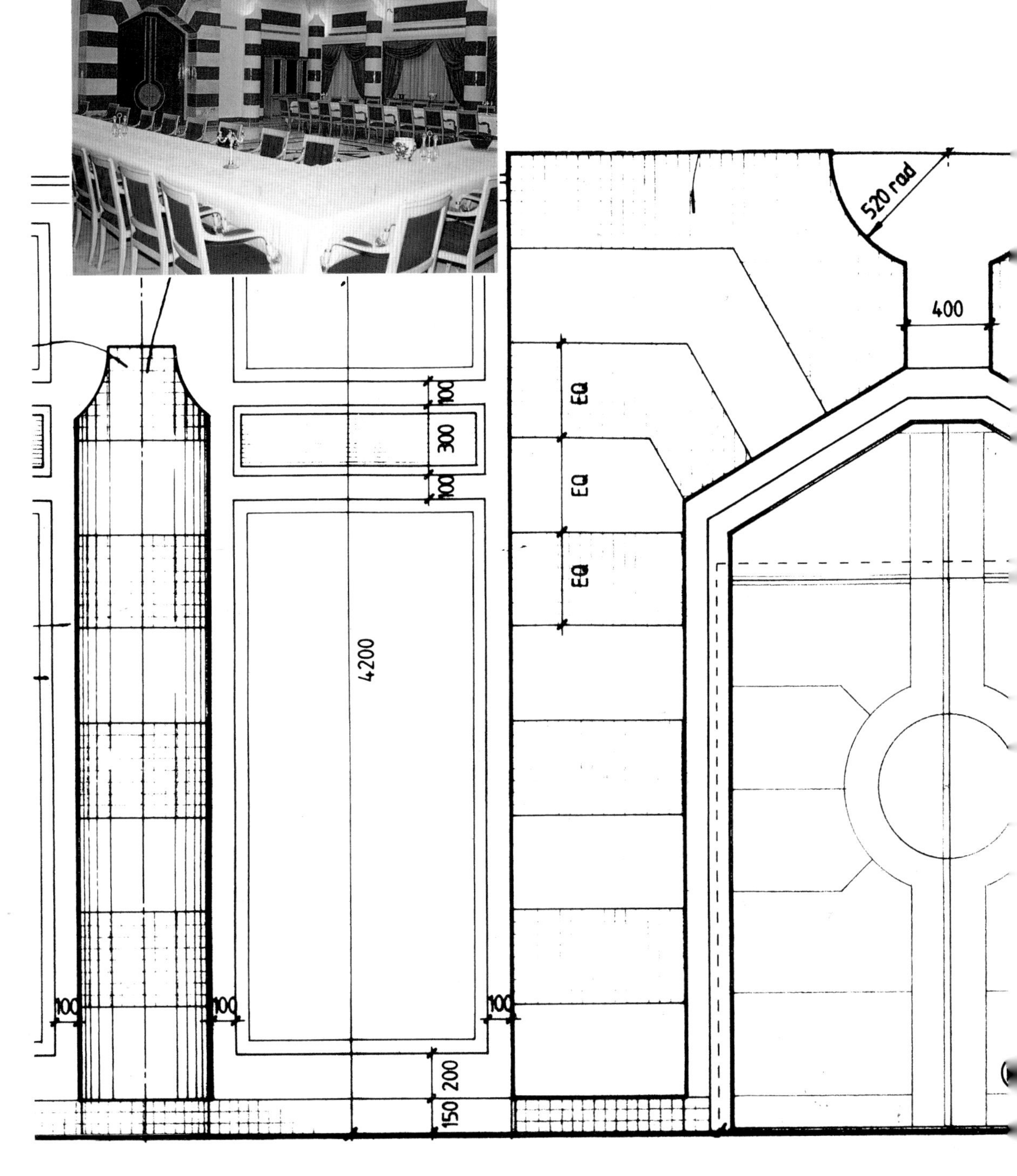

FAR LEFT *Bold shapes and colours give an unusual 'Egyptian post modern' feeling to this dining room.*

LEFT *The strong geometric feel of the room is echoed in the floor design.*

BELOW LEFT *The layout of the room must allow for circulation when all the seats are in use, enabling those serving the food to move freely round the table.*

BOTTOM *Sketch elevation. The banded panels are alternate white marble and deep blue glass mosaic.*

LEFT *The basic design of this dining room is very plain and simple, but the bold circular shape in the ceiling is highlighted with concealed lighting which adds drama and excitement to the whole area.*

OPPOSITE *Some dining areas are part of a larger living room. Here the floorcovering changes in the dining area to define where the table sits and to provide a more practical and easily maintained floor.*

LEFT *Here the dining area is separated from the rest of the room by low planters placed on each side, which also create the feeling of an entrance. The angled table makes the most of a rather small space, allowing a storage unit to fit into the corner.*

BELOW *A decorative table top adds interest to the otherwise blank surface of the table when it is not covered with a cloth. Central table bases are often better for small dining tables as they are set back out of the way.*

BEDROOMS

The bedroom can be more than just a place to sleep - it should also be an area to relax in, to prepare for the day ahead or wind down from the day just past. Comfort is the priority, not just physical comfort but also mental ease. The layout of the room, the selection of furniture, the colour scheme - all must combine to create the correct atmosphere.

Large bedrooms can become a personal living space, including areas of comfortable seating and sometimes even a desk for quiet working. This is particularly important in large families where more communal spaces may be busy and noisy. Even quite small rooms can be made to serve a dual purpose if they are carefully planned.

Careful planning is the key - the television should be placed so it can easily be watched from both the bed and the seating area, lights should be switched from beside the bed as well as from a central switch, storage must be versatile.

OPPOSITE *The position of the bed is important, an elaborately dressed canopy will emphasize the head of the bed so it becomes the focal point of the room.*

BELOW *Space should be allowed for bedside units and lamps on both sides of a double bed. It may also be worth considering switching the main room lights from the bed itself as well as from a central switch.*

RIGHT *Large bedrooms can take flamboyant 'Hollywood style' details. The bed canopy is a very strong feature that would look out of place in a smaller room, but here it imparts a sense of occasion and drama to an otherwise rather simple bedroom design.*

RIGHT *Bedrooms do not have to be in pastel shades, strong colours can work well in large rooms. Design sketch for a bedroom scheme.*

BELOW *The fabrics used in the scheme. The bedroom is part of a suite which includes a sitting room and dining room and the same colour scheme runs through all three rooms.*

BOTTOM *Detail of the carpet design, which picks up motifs and colours from the fabrics.*

BEDROOMS
Defining Areas

RIGHT *In this bedroom the bed is positioned to take advantage of the view from the picture window. Its position is defined by the circular detail in the ceiling above, which is echoed in the carpet design below.*

The sleeping area is separated from the seating area of the bedroom by a change in floor level and the steps curve to echo the strong circular shapes in ceiling and carpet. The built in unit behind the bed acts as headboard and also screens the bed from the breakfast alcove and desk.

BELOW *The floral motif in the carpet is carefully placed to emphasise the position of the bed even more and to create an area of interest in front of the tiny breakfast area. The flowers are taken from the major fabric used in the room.*

FAR RIGHT *The finished room.*

BEDROOMS
Featuring Shapes

A modern interpretation of Arabian Nights style. The exterior of the building is stretched tenting over a concrete shell and this theme is carried through into the interior. Lightweight silks were used inside to give the billowing effect of the ceiling and drapes.

BEDROOMS
Featuring Shapes

RIGHT *Specially designed fabrics and carpets can add an original touch to a room. The bed canopy pelmet picks up the geometric shape used in the fabric design.*

BELOW *The same custom fabric is used for the curtains.*

TOP FAR RIGHT *The initial fabric design with the co ordinating standard fabrics also used in the same scheme.*

CENTRE FAR RIGHT *The final fabric design as printed, with its border. The border was printed into the design every five metres, so the curtains could be made up with the border running along the bottom in a continuous band.*

BOTTOM FAR RIGHT *Detail of the carpet border which picks up some of the geometric shapes in the fabric design. A motif from the standard bedspread fabric has been used as the corner design for the carpet.*

BEDROOMS

Attention to Details

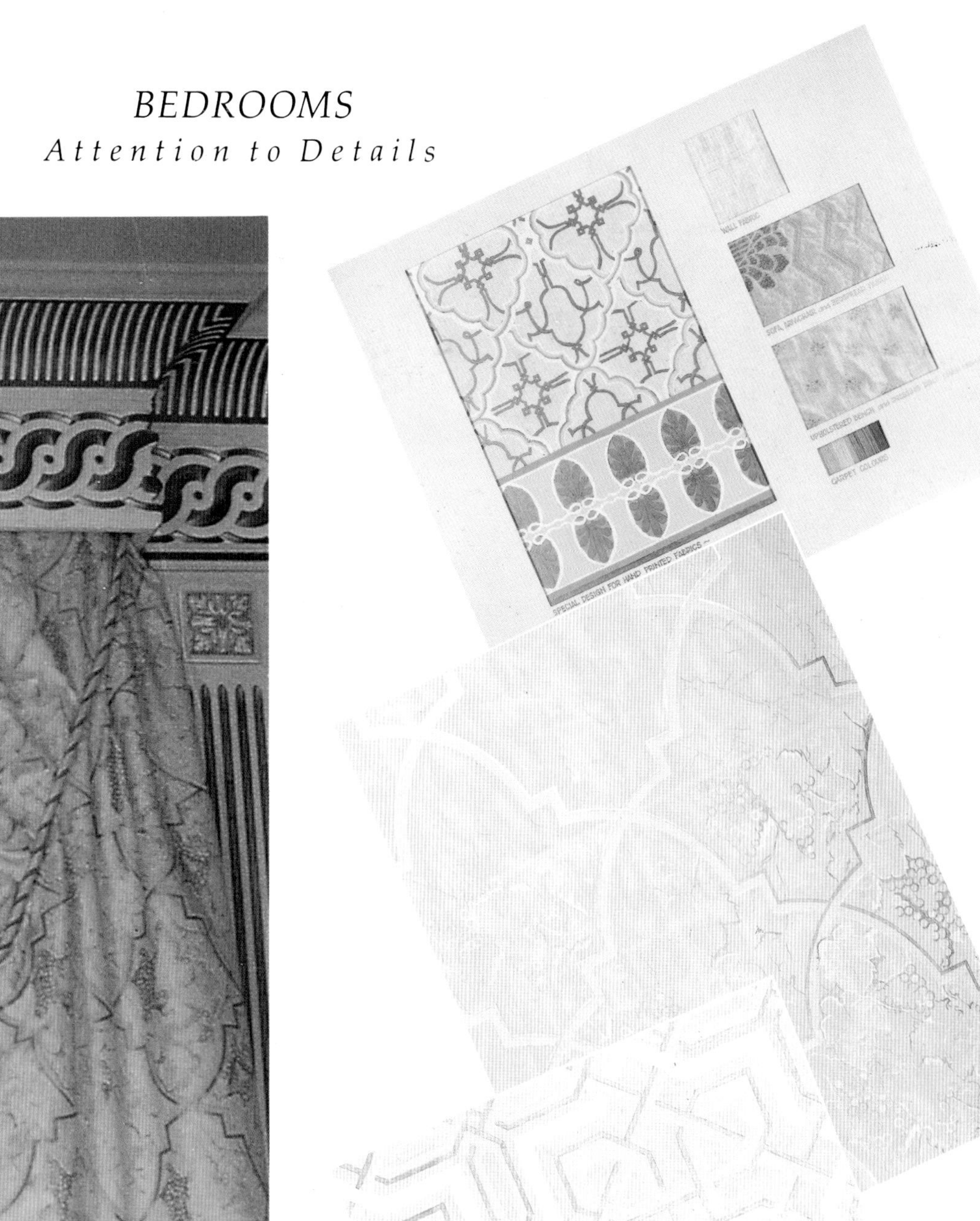

BATHROOMS

In design terms the bathroom has often been the most neglected room in the house. Recently, however, the emphasis has moved away from just providing a functional room to bathe in and towards creating a space in which the body can be pampered.

There are certain basic necessities that must be accommodated, but these can vary in style, shape and size enormously and there are a whole host of extras that can be added. A bath can be a standard oblong floor-standing model, or it can be round, square, sunken, raised, or made of mosaic or marble. The basin can be freestanding or inset into a counter top and can come in many shapes, sizes, materials and colours.

As well as these basics the bathroom is now often large enough to contain space for seating, and a wide range of other items - shower cubicles, whirlpool baths, steam rooms, heated towel rails, even exercise equipment.

OPPOSITE *Mirrors are very effective in a bathroom, particularly if it is small. They do not have to be plain in shape and can often be inset into the wall finish as a large panel.*

BELOW *The mirror above the hand basin should be as large as possible and also have adequate lighting.*

BATHROOMS
In the Grand Style

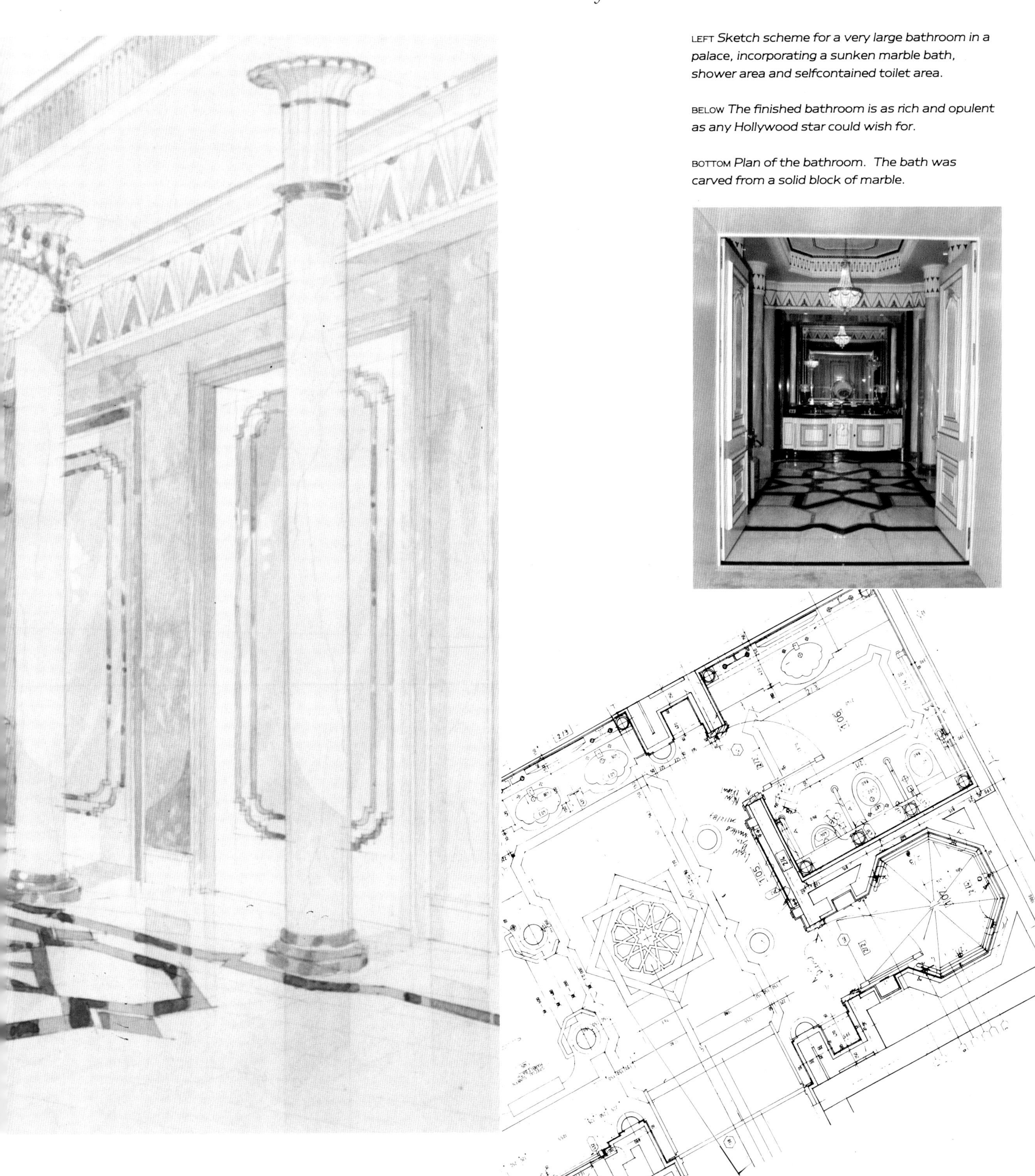

LEFT *Sketch scheme for a very large bathroom in a palace, incorporating a sunken marble bath, shower area and selfcontained toilet area.*

BELOW *The finished bathroom is as rich and opulent as any Hollywood star could wish for.*

BOTTOM *Plan of the bathroom. The bath was carved from a solid block of marble.*

RIGHT A standard corner bath becomes something special when it is set into a window alcove with stained glass panels and domed ceiling above.

BELOW Mosaic panels add colour to the walls, while bright cushions soften the starkness of the marble and mahogany bench.

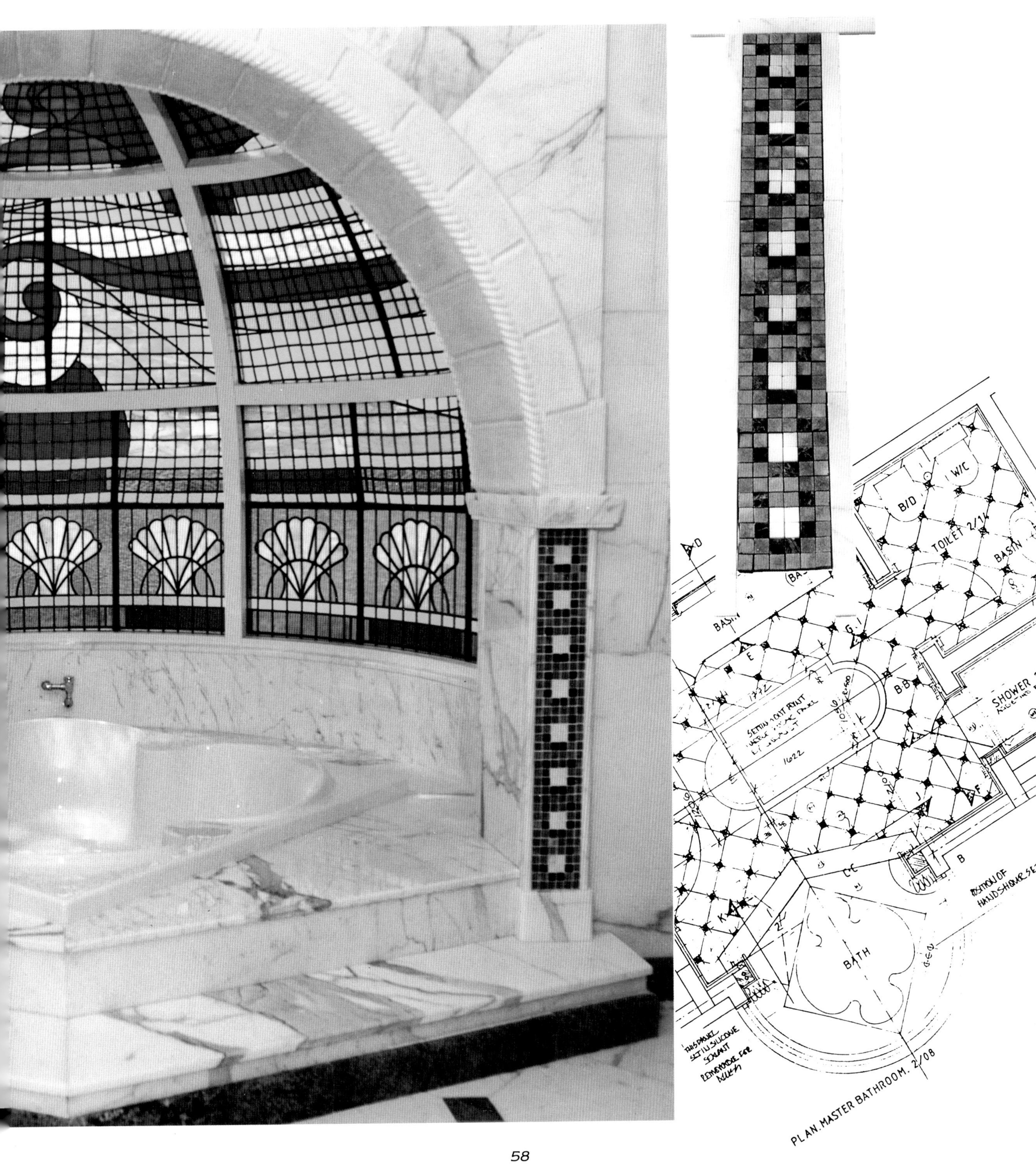
PLAN. MASTER BATHROOM. 2/08
BATH
SHOWER
TOILET
W/C
BASIN

BATHROOMS
Setting a Style

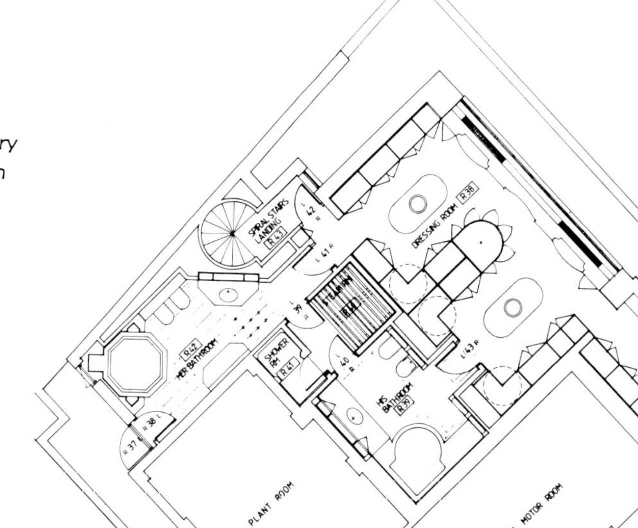

LEFT *Those with enough space can afford the luxury of 'his and hers' bathrooms. The lady's bathroom is decorated in pink and white marble, with pink accessories to give a very feminine room.*

BELOW *The man's room, in contrast, is in severe white marble and polished hardwood to give the aura of a gentleman's club.*

BATHROOMS

The Grandeur of Scale

BATHROOMS
The Grandeur of Scale

OPPOSITE *The sheer scale of large washrooms means that a dramatic design treatment can be very appropriate.*

LEFT *Washrooms often have to be fitted into odd shaped areas left over from other rooms. Well placed mirrors make this space look bigger, while their decorative arched shapes add extra interest to walls.*

BELOW LEFT *A much simpler treatment can be just as effective, as long as it still sympathetic in scale. For practical purposes the mirrors here could be much smaller, but tall mirrors fit better with the scale of the room.*

BELOW *A more modern treatment with a simple continuous mirror wall above the handbasins.*

BOTTOM *Large washrooms must be well planned so that essential items are in easy reach. Here each handbasin has its own mirror and towel.*

SWIMMING POOLS

To most people a private swimming pool is definitely a luxury, not only because of the cost involved but also because of the amount of space needed. The ideal pool area will not only include the swimming pool itself but also space for relaxing and for changing and showering nearby. Very large areas can be broken up into a series of interconnecting spaces to cover different functions, which will allow the design emphasis to be changed across the area – often quite dramatically.

Swimming pools no longer have to be simple geometric boxes – the basic shape can now be freeform to allow the pool to settle more naturally into the surrounding area. The sides and base can be decorated with tiles or mosaic designs to add interest to what can otherwise be rather boring flat expanses. These patterns will shift and change with the movement of water and light to create an ever varying design.

OPPOSITE *Outdoor pool in a tropical country with planting around the paved area to provide shade. The paved area is also on different levels to add interest.*

BELOW *Colonnade leading to the pool area. The slatted roof provides shade, but lets in a certain amount of sunlight to retain the outdoor feel. The slats also throw geometric patterns of shade and light on the otherwise plain whitewashed walls.*

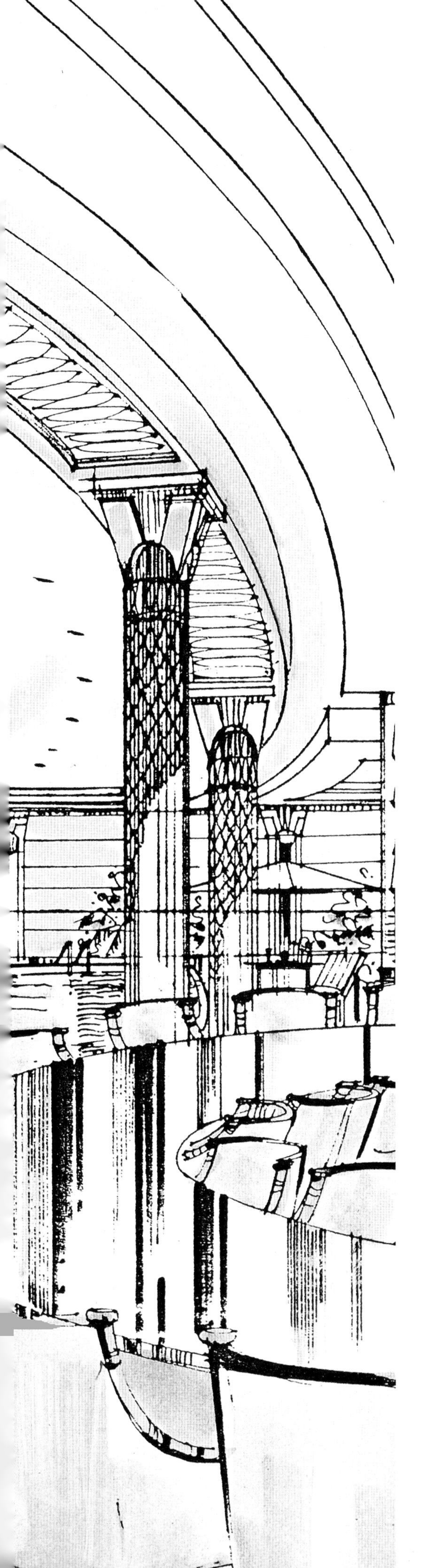

SWIMMING POOLS
Using Pattern

FAR LEFT Sketch design for the interior of a swimming pool. The necessary structural columns are decorated with mosaics, making them into a feature.

LEFT The sides and base of the oval pool are decorated with bouquets of flowers in mosaic.

BELOW LEFT Detail of the mosaic pattern.

BELOW Plan of the pool, which was built as an addition to an existing building. The shape was dictated by the constraints of the site.

BOTTOM Detail of the column decoration, fish scale shapes in graded colours.

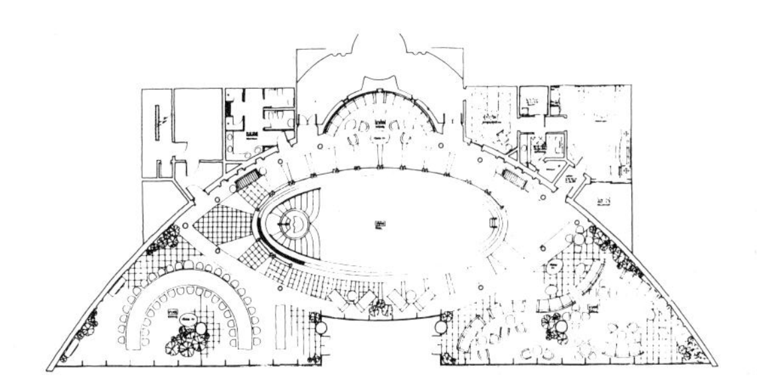

LEFT *Simple modern designs can work very well as long as strong detailing and interesting shapes are used. The circular jacuzzi at the end breaks up the oblong of the pool itself and the 'V' shaped vision panels in the doors add an unusual feature.*

BELOW *Detail of the jacuzzi area, with its wall fountain.*

BOTTOM *Plain modern furniture and a simple yet stylish wall mural are in keeping with the rest of the design.*

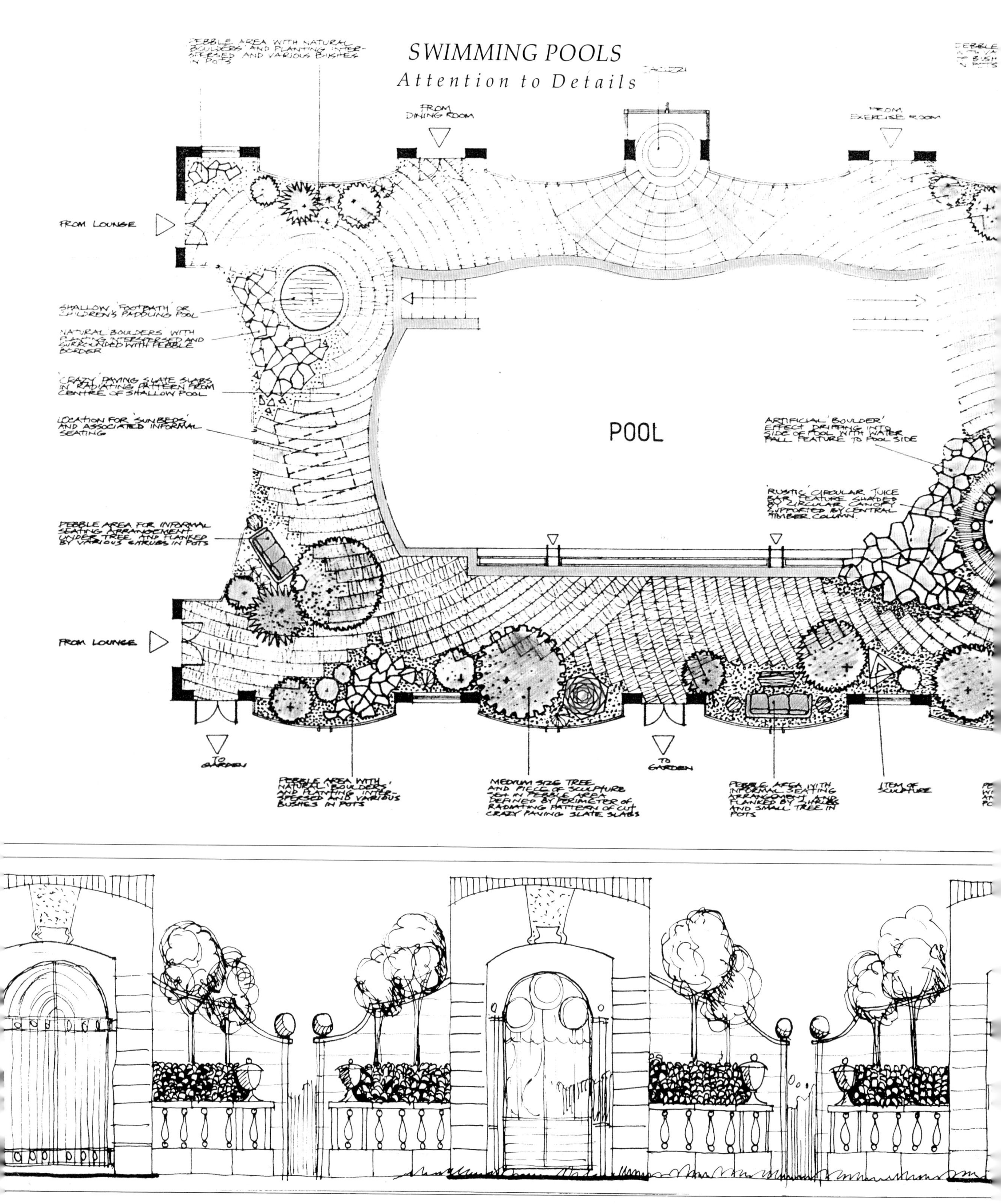
PEBBLE AREA WITH NATURAL BOULDERS AND PLANTING INTERSPERSED AND VARIOUS BUSHES IN POTS
JACUZZI
FROM DINING ROOM
FROM EXERCISE ROOM
FROM LOUNGE
SHALLOW 'FOOTBATH' OR CHILDREN'S PADDLING POOL
NATURAL BOULDERS WITH PLANTING INTERSPERSED AND SURROUNDED WITH PEBBLE BORDER
'CRAZY' PAVING SLATE SLABS IN RADIATING PATTERN FROM CENTRE OF SHALLOW POOL
LOCATION FOR 'SUNBEDS' AND ASSOCIATED INFORMAL SEATING
POOL
ARTIFICIAL 'BOULDER' EFFECT DRIPPING INTO SIDE OF POOL WITH WATER FALL FEATURE TO POOL SIDE
'RUSTIC' CIRCULAR JUICE BAR FEATURE SHADED BY CIRCULAR CANOPY SUPPORTED BY CENTRAL TIMBER COLUMN
PEBBLE AREA FOR INFORMAL SEATING ARRANGEMENT UNDER TREE AND FLANKED BY VARIOUS SHRUBS IN POTS
FROM LOUNGE
TO GARDEN
TO GARDEN
PEBBLE AREA WITH NATURAL BOULDERS AND PLANTING INTERSPERSED AND VARIOUS BUSHES IN POTS
MEDIUM SIZE TREE AND PIECE OF SCULPTURE SET IN PEBBLE AREA DEFINED BY PERIMETER OF RADIATING PATTERN OF CUT CRAZY PAVING SLATE SLABS
PEBBLE AREA WITH INFORMAL SEATING ARRANGEMENT AND FLANKED BY SHRUBS AND SMALL TREE IN POTS
ITEM OF SCULPTURE

A scheme for a walled and landscaped outdoor pool area, with suggestions for planting and ornaments. It is important that the whole area blends well if it is to look natural. Urns and sculpture among the foliage can add a suggestion of permanence and age, as long as they are in keeping with the design and in scale with the area. Seating is arranged in informal groups, often in the shade of trees.

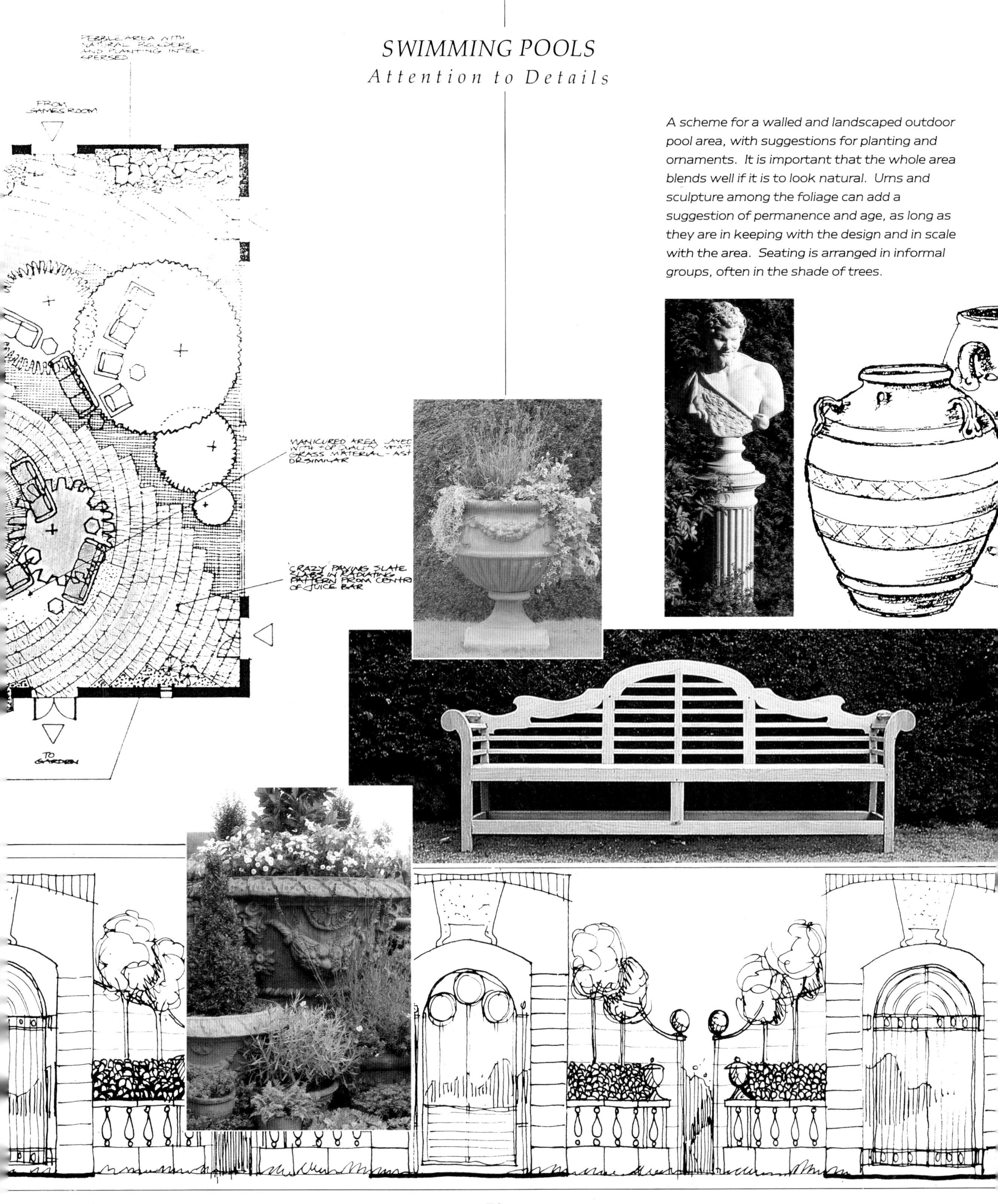

PANELLING

Plain walls were originally decorated with paintings or tapestries, but panelling - usually in wood - was introduced in the sixteenth century. At first panelling was invariably quite dark polished wood, but later light and dark woods or paint finishes were also used.

Modern panelling can be in many materials - wood, plasterwork, marble, mirror, mosaic, fabric - and ranges from the application of simple surface mouldings to elaborate carving and changes of level across the surface of the wall. Several different materials can be used together to make up the different elements of the panelling, wood mouldings around a central fabric panel for instance. Finishes to wood panelling vary enormously, ranging from polishing to special paint finishes. Unusual materials can be incorporated, such as gold leaf, inlaid metalwork or stones, mosaic panels.

Panelling does not have to be in simple rectangles, although some form of geometric shape will tend to work better because of the repetitive nature of the feature. The most important element is the proportion of the panelling, it must be correct both for the height of the room and the length of the panelling run.

OPPOSITE *Panelling in a formal salon.*
The panel centres are stretched fabric, while the applied decorative detail work is in bronze coloured resin.

BELOW *Panelled corridor in painted wood with a dragged finish and gold highlighting.*

LOUNGE

Highly decorative panelling with painted and dragged woodwork,elaborate panel decorations highlighted in gold leaf, complex cornice detailing and an inset mirrored area. Only a very large room can take such extravagant features without looking overdone. The furniture has been kept deliberately simple in style to counteract the exuberance of the walls.

PANELLING
Shapes and Styles

OPPOSITE RIGHT *Plain square panelling to a corridor in marble with surface mounted wood moulding. The colours and patterns in the marble make any extra decoration superfluous.*

OPPOSITE LEFT *Stepped mirror panels framed in bronze finished metal and inset into the marble wall of a bathroom.*

LEFT *Shaped panels of simple applied wood mouldings, set between plasterwork columns decorated with a mosaic centre panel.*

BELOW LEFT *Plain plaster panels alternate with pictorial mosaic scenes. The columns dividing the different panels are faced with mirror and have mosaic capitals.*

BELOW *The mosaic panel adds colour and interest to the walls, echoing the colours in the furnishing fabrics.*

PANELLING
Using Pattern

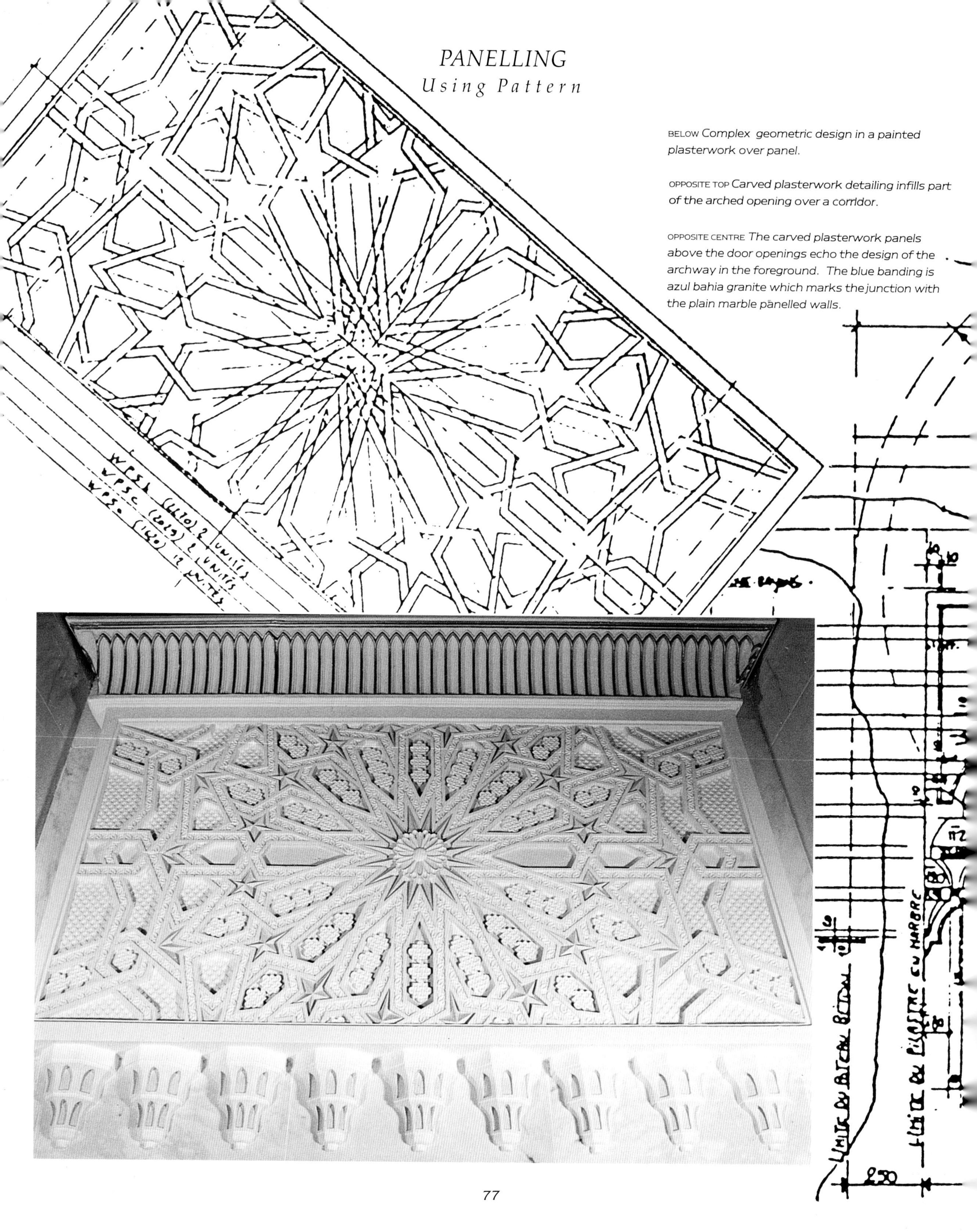

BELOW *Complex geometric design in a painted plasterwork over panel.*

OPPOSITE TOP *Carved plasterwork detailing infills part of the arched opening over a corridor.*

OPPOSITE CENTRE *The carved plasterwork panels above the door openings echo the design of the archway in the foreground. The blue banding is azul bahia granite which marks the junction with the plain marble panelled walls.*

PANELLING

Using Pattern

PANELLING
Attention to Details

PANELLING

Attention to Details

OPPOSITE TOP *Detail of a wall panel with inlay work in contrasting woods.*

OPPOSITE CENTRE *Wall panel veneered to use the grain of the wood to make patterns and shapes and a wall panel with inlay work in contrasting wood veneers.*

OPPOSITE BOTTOM *Panel moulding with inset bronze coloured resin details.*

BELOW *Details of panel corners using carved mouldings, resin inlay work and textured finishes to create different designs.*

DOORS

Doorways are openings into another area, the threshold between two possibly very different places. Although the design of the door must generally coordinate with the style of the room, there is still scope for interesting features and finishes.

Decoration on doors generally has to take into account handles, locks and hinges, so these are often made into features. The metalwork bands which sometimes extend across the doors from hinges were originally to add strength, but are now usually merely decorative.

Door openings do not have to be a simple rectangle, they can be arched or asymmetrically shaped if the design of the building calls for it. The door which fits in to such a shaped opening can either have an overpanel to fill in part of the shape, making the door itself more or less rectangular, or can match the shape of the opening. Very large door openings often need smaller doors within them for practical reasons, in which case it is important that the doors and surrounding infill areas are carefully designed in proportion and to blend with one another.

OPPOSITE *Double doors with shaped panels, finished in cream paintwork with gold highlights on mouldings and architrave detailing.*

BELOW *Detail of a pair of door handles, the design on the plate echoing the decorative banding round the panels.*

RIGHT *Three sets of double doors in bookmatched burr walnut with bronze decorative panels, leading into a state dining room. The main central pair are the full three metre height of the opening, the two side pairs are slightly smaller with overpanels. The circular arch detail in the panelling reflects an architectural motif used in the building.*

BELOW RIGHT *Detail of the bronze handles and bronze decorative banding to the central door .*

0
150
0

OPPOSITE *Exterior doors clad in bronze sheet with cast bronze decorative panels.*

LEFT *Square panelled doors with a simple moulding detail and architraves.*

BELOW *Highly decorated doors with complex shaped mouldings, textured panels, carved motifs and an oval antique mirror detail in the lower panel.*

BOTTOM *Square panelled doors with carved decorative motif incorporated in the moulding of the top panel. Wider gold banded architraves and a decorative overpanel make the doors look more imposing.*

DOORS
Using Pattern

RIGHT *Entrance doors to a mosque with a stained glass overpanel.*

OPPOSITE *The design for the entrance doors, which uses a cast bronze decorative framework applied to a wooden door, the spaces between the bands filled with carved teak panels.*

OPPOSITE BOTTOM RIGHT *Designs for teak entrance doors, using a combination of carved wood and cast bronze decorative panels.*

DOORS

Using Pattern

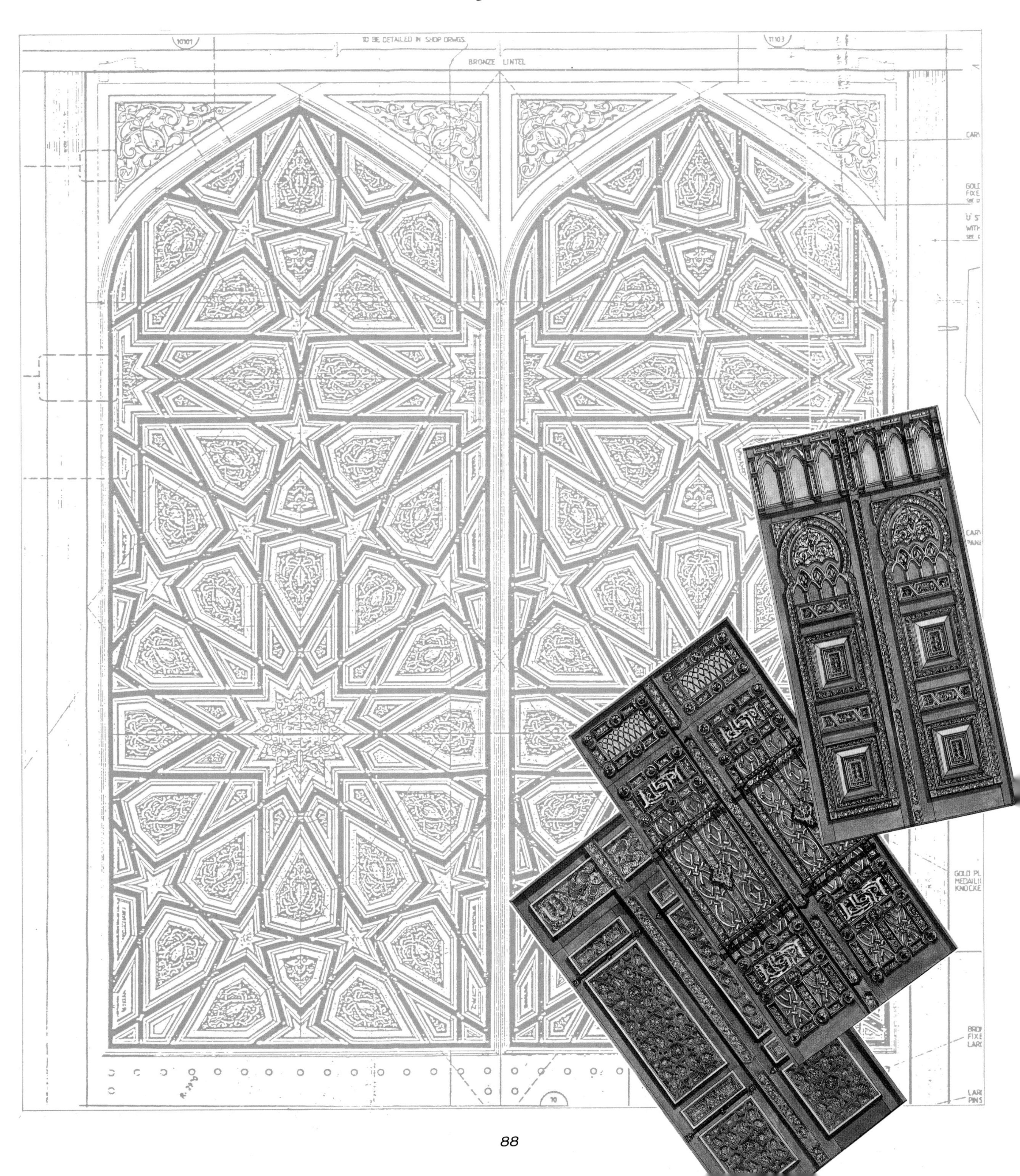

DOORS

Creating a Focus

RIGHT *Exterior doors in wood with bronze detailing.*

BELOW *The main exterior doors to the building are the focus of the front elevation. Here the shape of the porch ceiling leads the eye directly towards the double doors, which are placed symmetrically between two windows.*

OPPOSITE *Exterior door in a pointed arch. The shapes created by the mouldings echo the arch and the central pattern continues up into the overpanel to make the doors visually appear bigger than they are.*

DOORS
Creating a Focus

RIGHT *Glass doors divide a space physically but not visually. They let in light, but can still have decorative features. Pair of double glass doors with sand blasted pattern and applied gold banding.*

BELOW *Detail of the decoration.*

LEFT *These doors into a bar have cross work metal glazing bars to add interest to the clear glass vision panels.*

BELOW LEFT *Folding doors dividing a living and dining room. The top panels are frosted glass, the bottom oval panels are 'antique' coloured mirror.*

BELOW *Glass panel exterior doors with a combination of sand blasted and gold decoration.*

COLUMNS

Columns originally provided supplementary support for the roof or ceiling, allowing it to span a larger area. Modern building methods allow a much wider span to be achieved without columns, but they are often still included as a decorative feature. Full or half columns can be used around the edge of a room to frame a doorway or window, or to break up a long run of panelling into sections.

A column typically comes in three basic sections, the base, the pier or shaft, and the capital at the top. The base is usually fairly simple in design, it is wider than the pier and marks the junction with the floor. The pier itself can come in many shapes, round, fluted, square, octagonal, but again it is often simple in design.

The capital has two purposes - to provide a larger area than the pier from which the arch can spring, and to form a decorative joint between the pier and the arch. Capitals are often very rich in decoration, perhaps gilded or painted to contrast with the simplicity of the pier beneath.

OPPOSITE *Columns in marble with classical composite capitals. The composite style is a combination of the Corinthian and the Ionic orders.*

BELOW *Detail of a composite capital.*

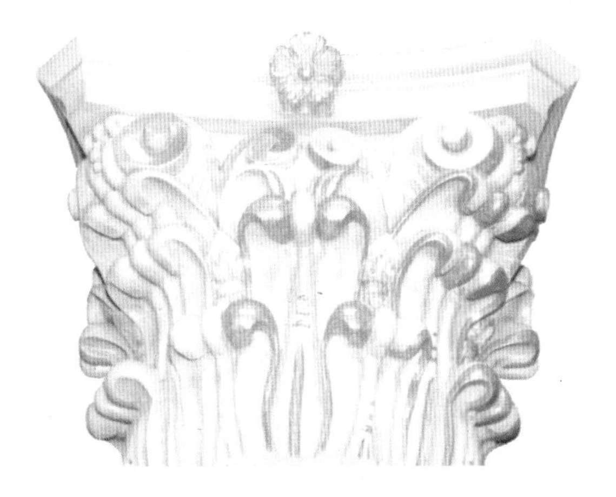

COLUMNS
Creating a Theme

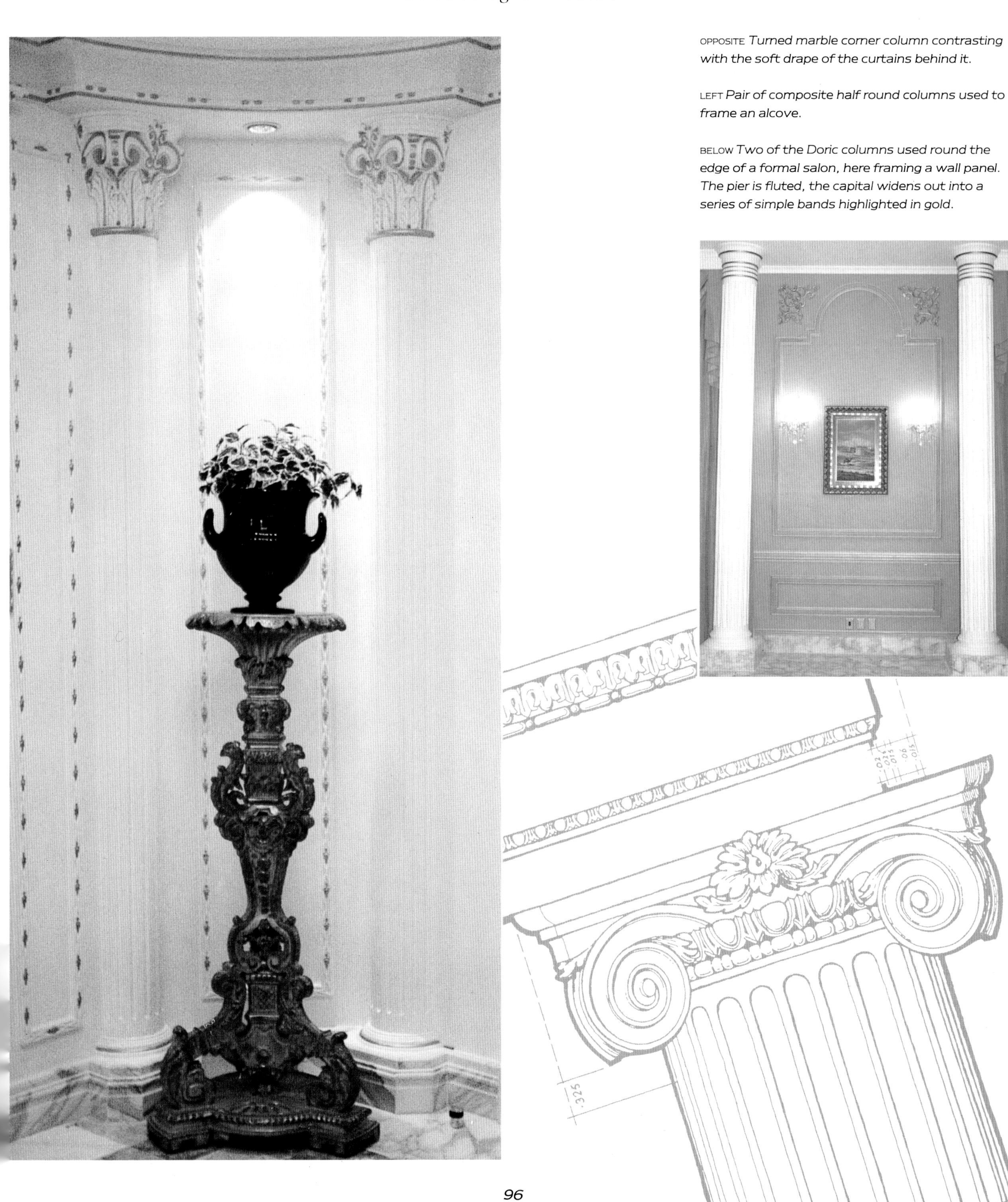

OPPOSITE *Turned marble corner column contrasting with the soft drape of the curtains behind it.*

LEFT *Pair of composite half round columns used to frame an alcove.*

BELOW *Two of the Doric columns used round the edge of a formal salon, here framing a wall panel. The pier is fluted, the capital widens out into a series of simple bands highlighted in gold.*

RIGHT *Columns do not have to be designed in the classical style. Detail of two columns framing a door in an entrance hall. The plain pier contrasts with the elaborate shell design of the capital.*

BELOW RIGHT *View down the entrance hall, the series of columns emphasises the shape of the area and focuses attention towards the doors at the far end.*

BELOW *Mosaic clad columns surrounding a swimming pool.*

BOTTOM *The pair of columns in the corner of this room have a barley sugar twist base in dark marble, a plain octagonal marble pier and a simple polished wood capital.*

OPPOSITE *A pair of columns in marble, rising out of a marble plinth. The capital is decorated with a geometric design in bronze finish.*

RIGHT *Modern strongly geometric column in painted fibrous plaster, incorporating an uplight.*

BELOW *Alternate bands of white marble and deep blue glass mosaic tiles decorate the piers of these columns. Again they incorporate lighting to uplight the area.*

OPPOSITE *Decorative pilasters on either side of a hand basin also support small wall lights.*

OPPOSITE BOTTOM *These small quarter columns on either side of a hand basin recess incorporate light fittings within the pier.*

RIGHT *Detail of a composite capital.*

OPPOSITE *The five classical orders - from the right: Tuscan, Doric, Ionic, Corinthian and Composite.*

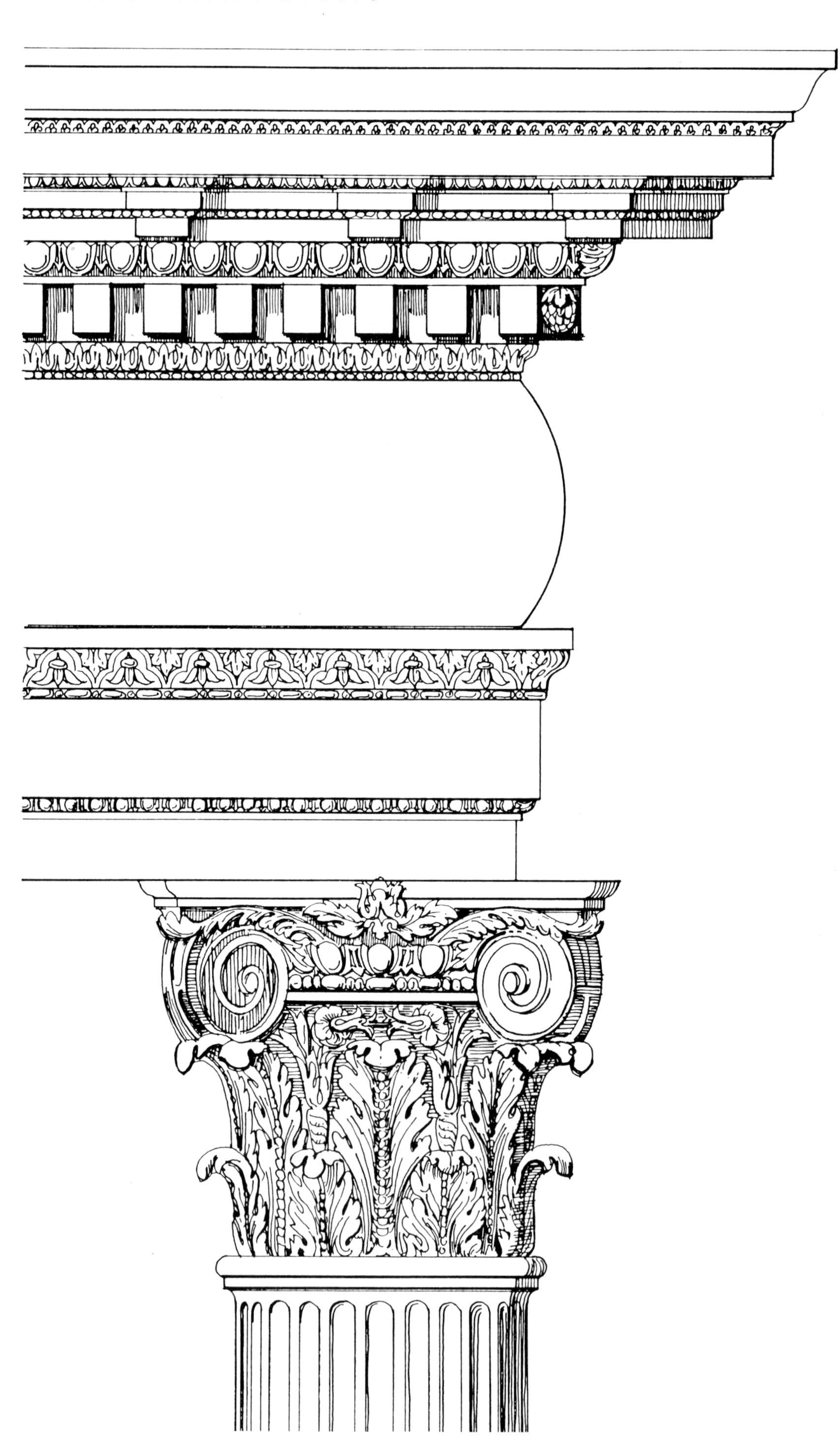

Donnés à Pille fils cadet, le 14 7bre 1835
Par Deveria Père —

CEILINGS

The flat plaster ceiling only became common in the late sixteenth century. Before this ceilings were normally stone or wood and were vaulted or arched from columns as this was the only way large areas could be spanned. The flat ceiling was a novelty and it was not until much later in the eighteenth century that ceiling decoration came into its own again and the flat surfaces were decorated; in relief with plaster mouldings or painted with patterns or murals.

The ceiling is often neglected now, considered merely as a convenient place to put lights. There is no reason why the ceiling should be a simple flat expanse though and there are a wide range of materials and effects that can be used to add more interest.

Domed ceilings can be a very special feature, adding extra height to a particular area. They can also be heavily decorated to accentuate their shape. If an area has a very high ceiling overall, varying ceiling levels can be introduced and these can be accentuated with lighting to create a dramatic effect.

OPPOSITE *View up from the first floor gallery into the dome above a double height area in the centre of an entrance hall. The plaster relief decoration on the surface of the dome is highlighted in gold.*

BELOW *Ceiling rose in relief plaster work, the pattern accentuated with colour. The colour is hand painted after the plasterwork is installed.*

RIGHT *This dome has been decorated with elaborate relief patterns in painted plasterwork. Again all the decorative work has been done in situ.*

FAR RIGHT *The geometric patterns had to be adjusted to follow the curve of the dome, both horizontally and vertically.*

RIGHT *Elaborate ceiling design with changes of level, textured areas, concealed lighting and a decorative chandelier.*

BELOW RIGHT *A ceiling with simple recessed areas, the edges highlighted with concealed fluorescent lighting. In the centre the ceiling steps up to its full height, allowing space for a much larger chandelier than those round the edges.*

BELOW *Decorative raised plaster work border around the edge of a room, incorporating pin spot downlights at intervals. The downlight itself is made to appear as part of the decorative motif.*

OPPOSITE *Elaborate ceiling design with several changes of level. Again each level is highlighted around its perimeter with concealed lighting. The AC grille runs round the edge of one of the recesses, becoming part of the decorative design.*

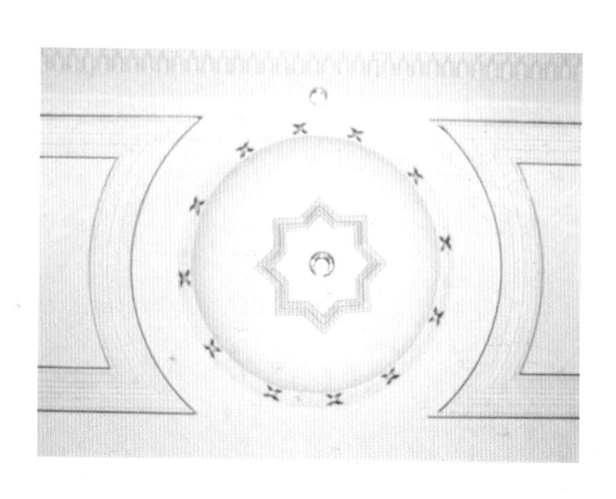

CEILINGS
Creating Features

CEILINGS
Creating Features

LEFT *All types of pendant light fittings look better if they spring from some sort of decorative point in the ceiling and the ceiling rose used to be an accepted decorative feature. Design drawing for a plaster ceiling rose.*

BELOW LEFT *The finished ceiling rose in situ. The motifs in raised plaster have been highlighted in gold.*

BELOW RIGHT *Raised plaster ceiling rose in a complex geometric design, highlighted in soft pastel colours. The downlights around the outside are to accentuate the sparkle of the crystals in the chandelier.*

BOTTOM LEFT *Acanthus leaf ceiling rose highlighted in gold.*

BOTTOM RIGHT *Instead of a ceiling rose, this chandelier is suspended from the centre of a miniature dome.*

CEILINGS

Attention to Details

CEILINGS
Attention to Details

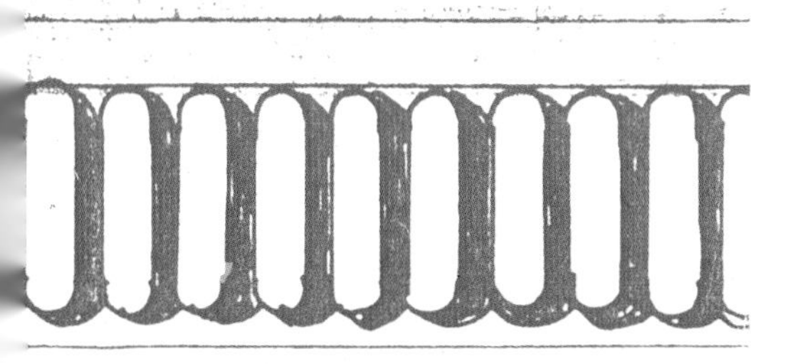

OPPOSITE TOP *Complex geometric cornice design, in relief plasterwork, highlighted with colour.*

OPPOSITE CENTRE *Simple cornices can be very effective. Here the cornice has a pair of gold lines which also visually bridge the gap between the ceiling and the top of the column, increasing the importance of the column capital.*

OPPOSITE BOTTOM *Plasterwork cornice with simple gold coachlines.*

FAR LEFT *Design for a repeating shell motif cornice.*

TOP LEFT *The finished shell motif cornice in relief plasterwork, highlighted in gold.*

CENTRE LEFT *The decorative cornice steps round a column detail in the corner of the room.*

BELOW *Decorative plasterwork cornice round the opening in the floor between two levels. The lines of simple repetitive motifs build up to quite a complex pattern.*

BELOW *Traditional plasterwork ceilings are not the only option. Open timber slats run between X-shaped plasterwork beams, allowing light through from the glass skylight above. Around the edge is a continuous crystal prism chandelier.*

BOTTOM *Kitchen ceiling panel of frosted perspex panels on a wooden grid. The panel has fluorescent lighting behind it, so it acts as ceiling and light fitting.*

OPPOSITE *Here the ceiling has geometric ribs in deep relief, leading the eye to the central glass dome.*

MARBLE

Marble has been used to decorate floors and walls throughout the ages. It has been cut into sheets and used as paving or wall panels, carved into column heads, mouldings or decorative friezes, cut into tiny pieces and used in mosaic patterns. It is hardwearing enough to be used on both interior and exterior surfaces and comes in a variety of colours and tones.

Some types of marble are fairly evenly coloured throughout, others have coloured streaks or patterns that can vary tremendously - even from different areas of the same quarry. These natural variations can be used to create interesting effects and designs without the addition of any artificial colouring.

Modern technology means that marble can now be cut into much thinner sheets than was possible in earlier years, thus eliminating weight problems in some applications as well as cutting costs. Although this has meant that marble is now much more widely used, it still manages to convey an impression of classic elegance and enduring stability.

OPPOSITE *Marble lends itself readily to being cut into geometric shapes. Inlaid floor pattern in statuario venato and calacatta francia with cremo valencia strips, marbre du roi key squares and verde St Dennis border.*

BELOW *Table top in cremo valencia, with rosso franci border and central motif in rosso levanto and statuario.*

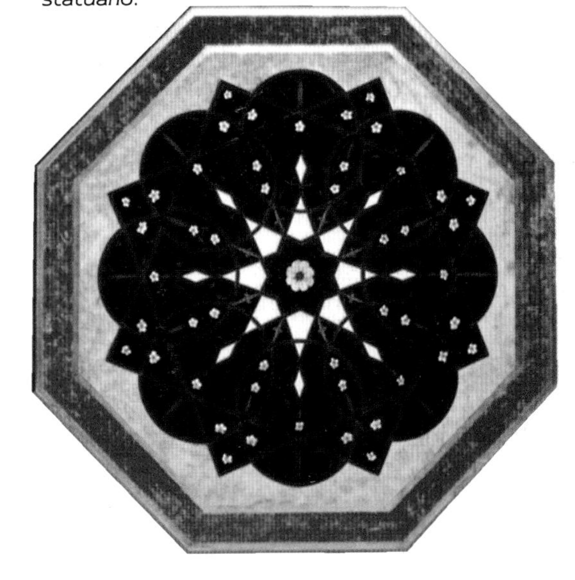

MARBLE
The Grandeur of Scale

LEFT *Hardwearing enough to withstand most weather conditions, marble makes an excellent exterior cladding. Exterior of a building clad in panels of bianco carrara, with a scored finish done by bush hammering in straight lines.*

BELOW *Overall view of the building.*

BOTTOM *The bianco carrara marble strips surrounding doors and windows are polished, while the darker contrast strips are azul bahia granite.*

RIGHT *Natural variations in colour can be used to create interesting effects and designs without the addition of any artificial colouring. Corridor with bookmatched panels of statuario venato on the walls. The columns are arabescato, with sienna giallo contrast set into the skirting. The dark panel framing is polished wood, set on the marble.*

BELOW *Coordinating wall panels and floor decoration. The background is calacatta with green verde alpi contrast, while the pattern is made of breccia pernice and breccia oniciata.*

FAR RIGHT CENTRE *Geometric floor pattern using a background of botticino with light green piel serpiente, dark green verde aver and red rosso levanto.*

FAR RIGHT BOTTOM *Marble wall panels in cremo delicato with azul bahia granite banding.*

FIRE
052
TRANCE LOBBY

The marble pattern echoes the shapes of the arches in the area. Walls in cremo delicato with verde alpi banding, floor in statuario with verde aver and breccia pernice banding and botticino panels. The central pattern is marble mosaic in all colours.

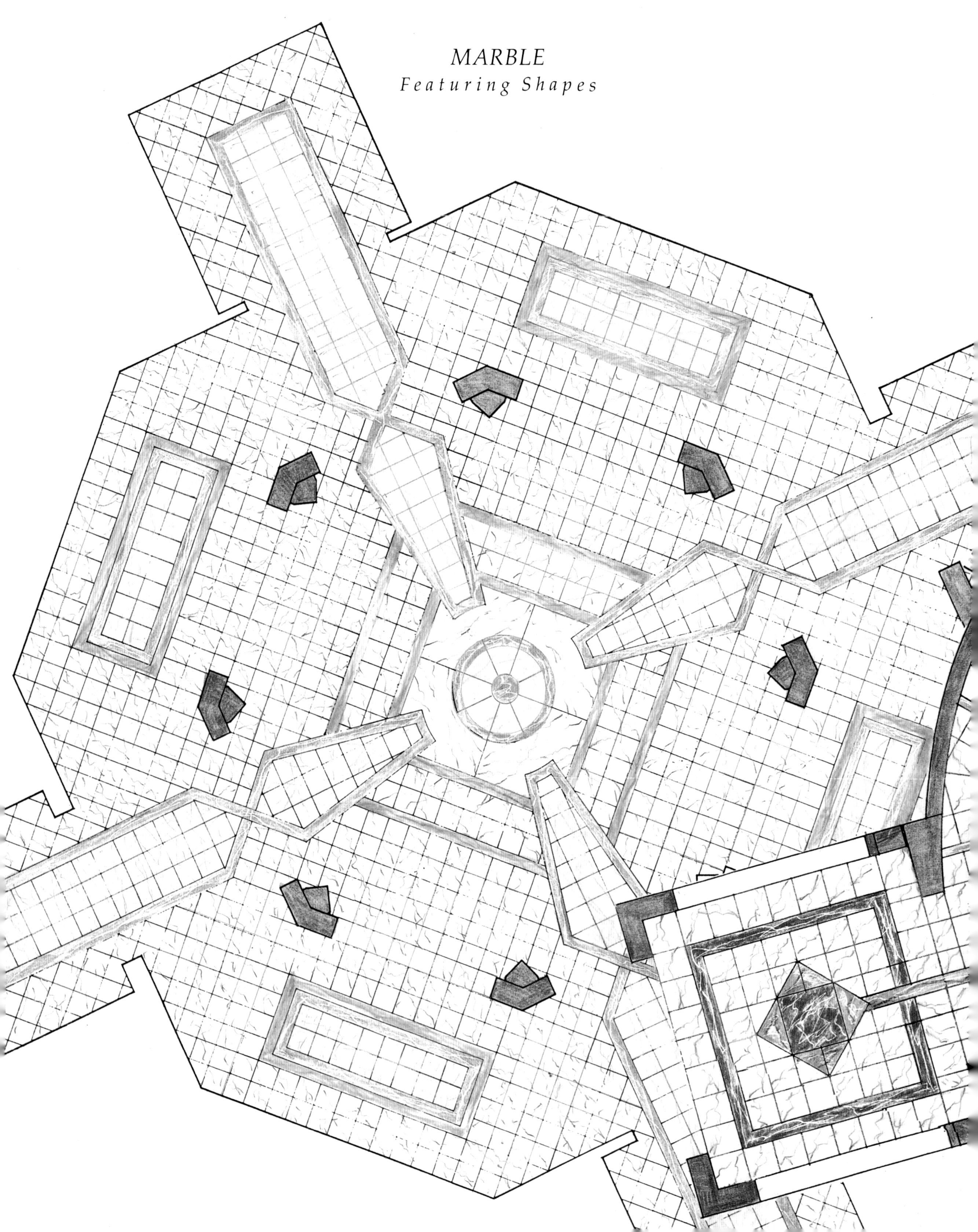
MARBLE
Featuring Shapes

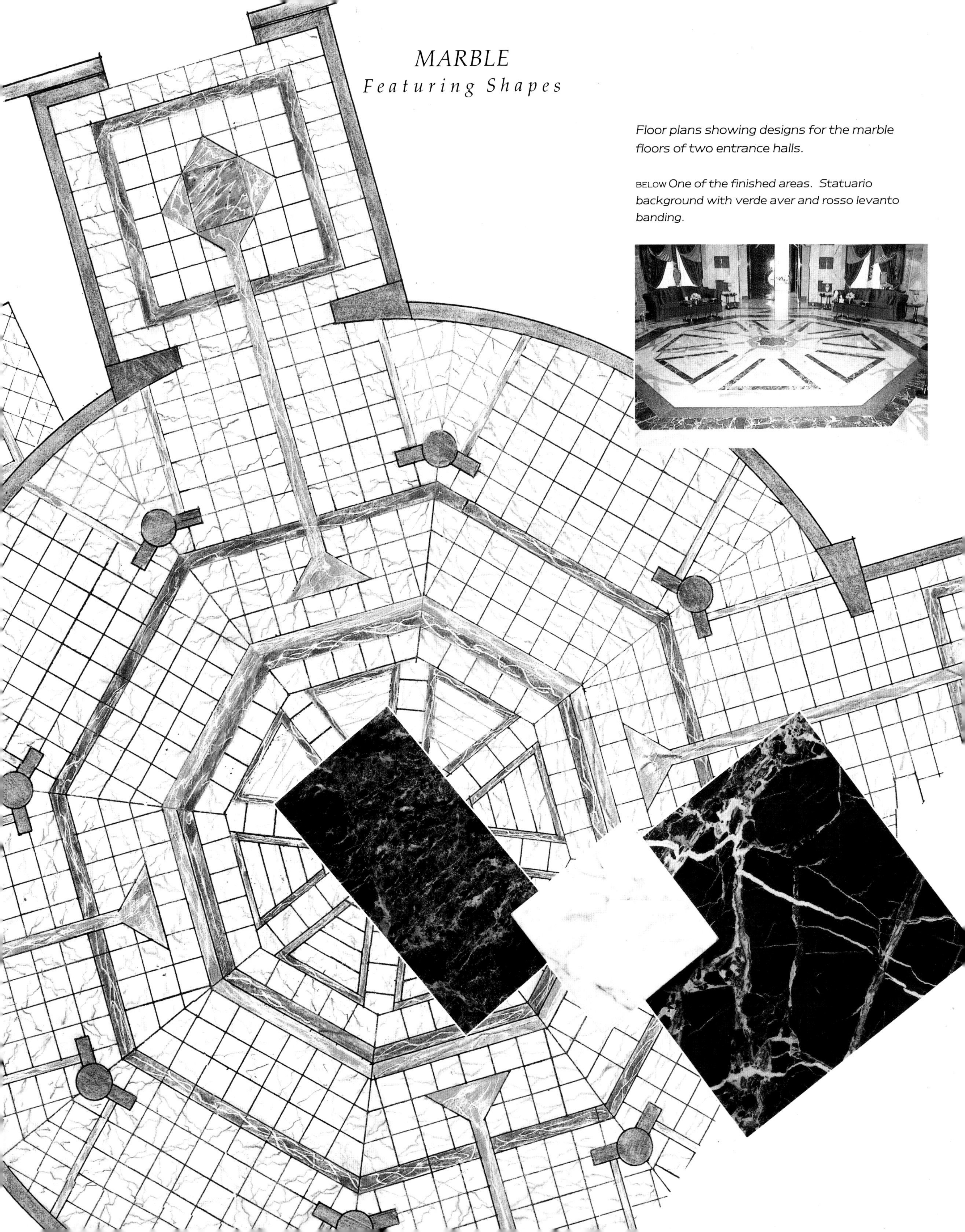

MARBLE
Featuring Shapes

Floor plans showing designs for the marble floors of two entrance halls.

BELOW One of the finished areas. Statuario background with verde aver and rosso levanto banding.

LEFT *Design for a handcut marble mosaic pattern to be used as the centre piece for a marble floor design.*

BELOW *The finished mosaic panel in situ.*

BOTTOM *Details of the design. The background is statuario with inlay in rosa aurora, verde laguna, azul bahia, verde alpi, sienna giallo, and rosso levanto.*

TURBO V-20

Marble is quarried in blocks and then either sliced into sheets for cladding or carved into shapes. The sheets were originally cut from the block by hand and were therefore fairly thick, but the development of modern technology means that much thinner sheets can be achieved. This also means that marble tiles are now available which are much cheaper to use for cladding than marble panels.

Although the material is hard some types are also very brittle, so panels must be backed with glass fibre and resin to stop them breaking into pieces - particularly when they are used for table or worktops.

The marble dust which is a byproduct of the cutting and polishing process can be combined with resin and cast, so detailed 'carved' shapes can be made without the laborious process of hand carving.

Marble can be used rough, or there are a variety of finishes which can be applied to the surface; it can be polished, flamed, hammered, sandblasted or etched.

OPPOSITE TOP LEFT *Applying a bush hammered finish to a shaped wall panel piece.*

OPPOSITE TOP RIGHT *Hand finishing a column capital which has been cast in marble dust and resin.*

OPPOSITE BOTTOM LEFT *Polishing and shaping cut pieces by hand.*

OPPOSITE BOTTOM RIGHT *Cutting shapes from a marble sheet.*

RIGHT *Laying out a wall panel design to check the shapes and colours.*

SERVAL
27

MOSAICS

The art of making patterns in mosaic dates from the 8th century BC and many early examples are still in existence due to the hardwearing nature of the materials used. Mosaic designs have been made from pieces of natural stone, coloured glass, ceramics and resins and the tiny component parts mean that complex and detailed patterns can be achieved. The name 'mosaic' comes from the Latin musaicum - meaning a work of patience worthy of the muses.

A mosaic can be in subtle, natural or bright, clear colours depending on the material chosen. The natural variation of colour and tone in materials such as marble can be used to great effect, while modern colouring techniques for glass and ceramics provide a wide range of stronger colours. The material is suitable for flooring as well as wall panels, for use inside as well as out.

Designs can vary from naturalistic pictures, to geometric patterns, to freeform shapes and colours. Flat surfaces are not required, mosaic works just as well round curves and angles - its versatility as an applied decoration is enormous.

OPPOSITE *Floor in marble mosaic in a Paris shopping centre, a restoration of an existing 18th century design.*

BELOW *Floor panel for a bathroom in ceramic mosaic.*

LEFT *Entrance hall with a floor of marble inset with marble mosaic panels.*

ABOVE *Detail of a central marble mosaic design.*

BELOW *Various geometric marble mosaic panels, which will be used in marble floor designs as the central feature.*

LEFT *The sides and bottom of a swimming pool can be a plain featureless expanse, but here a design in glass mosaic adds interest and colour.*

BELOW *Alternative designs for the same pool. Glass mosaics offer a wide range of bright colours.*

OPPOSITE *This abstract design in bright colours for the walls round a fountain in Paris was taken from a painting by F. Mitrofanoff and executed in glass mosaics.*

FRANCE
MITROFANOFF

FAR LEFT CENTRE *Detail of a wall panel design laid out for checking before installation. The picture is seen in reverse because the tiles are fixed upside down to a facing sheet. The side which is facing upwards here will be applied to the wall, then the facing sheet which is holding the tiles together will be peeled away and they will be grouted into place.*

FAR LEFT BOTTOM *The finished wall panel in situ. The informal pictorial scene is made of glass mosaic tiles.*

LEFT *Formal geometric design wall panels in glass mosaic add an area of pattern and colour to simple white marble walls. The colours in the mosaic pick up the upholstery and the floor banding.*

MOSAICS
Creating Features

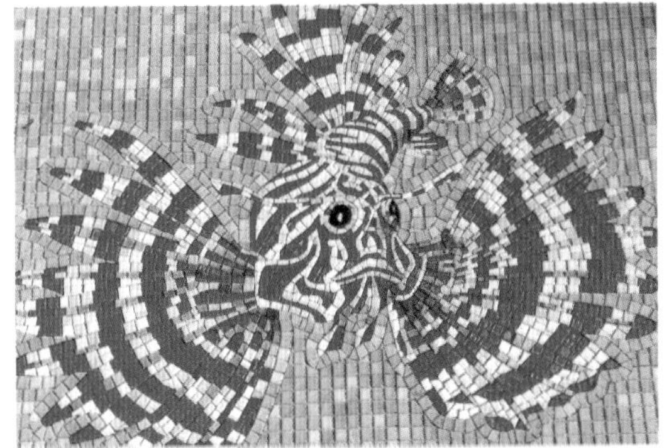

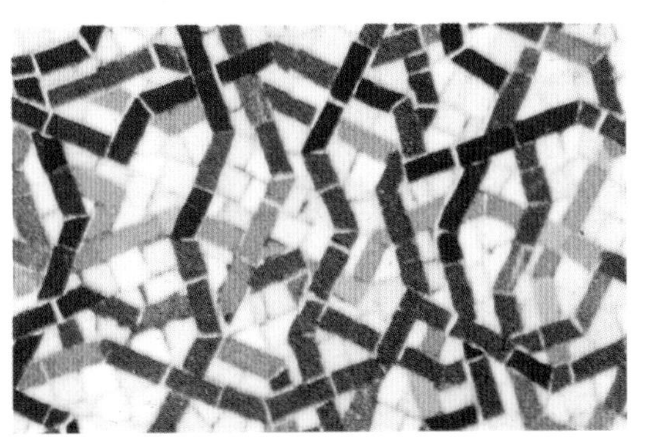

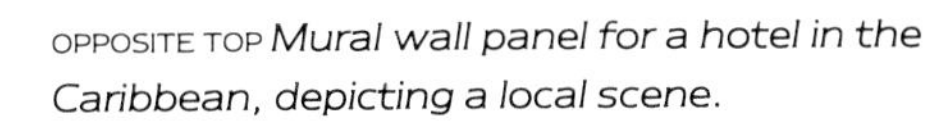

OPPOSITE TOP *Mural wall panel for a hotel in the Caribbean, depicting a local scene.*

OPPOSITE BOTTOM *Detail of fishing boats from another panel on the same project.*

CENTRE *Detail of a large abstract design in bright clear colours.*

LEFT *Two details of glass mosaic fish on the sides of a swimming pool, part of a design which gives an impression of being under the sea.*

BELOW LEFT *Detail of a pictorial wall panel of a swan in glass mosaic, from a painting by Xavier Degans.*

BOTTOM LEFT *Abstract design for a wall panel in glass mosaic, from a painting by Grataloup.*

BELOW *Wall panel in a garden, a trompe l'oeil picture of a fountain in glass mosaic.*

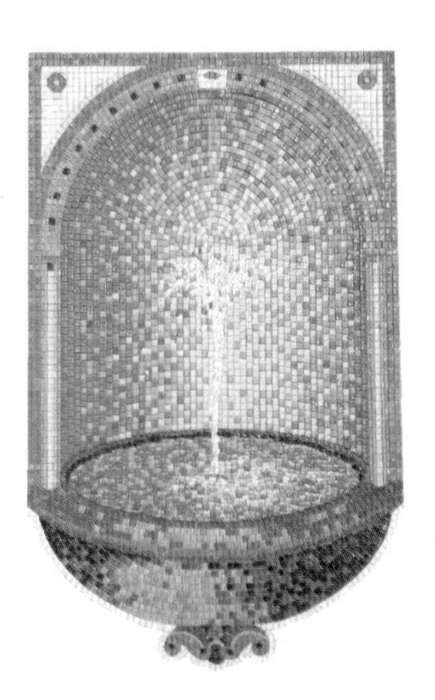

FAR LEFT *Zelige is traditional Middle Eastern mosaic made from tiny shaped ceramic tiles. Here it is used to clad a fountain in the centre of a courtyard.*

LEFT *Coloured design drawing for a zelige mosaic.*

BELOW LEFT *Floor panel in zelige mosaic. The tiles come in many shapes and colours, so the variety of geometric designs that can be achieved is almost endless.*

BOTTOM *Detail of part of a design.*

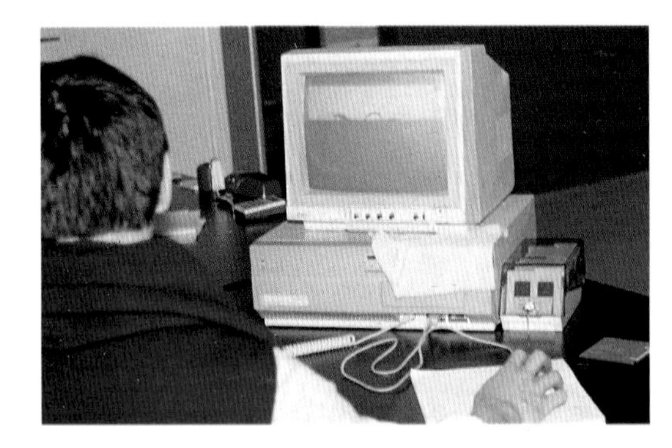

Mosaics can be made from many materials, including natural stone, coloured glass, ceramics and resins.

Stone mosaic is usually either marble or limestone with only the natural colours in the material available. The cubes of material are cut by hand from thin strips of stone which have been sliced by machine from a slab.

Ceramic mosaic is either in the natural earth colours of the clay or the tiny tiles can be glazed in bright colours as in zelige.

Glass mosaics also come in two types. First is the glass paste type, which are coloured all through and come in a limited colour range. It is difficult to match colours exactly between batches, so some variation in colour is inevitable. With the glass enamel type the powdered colour is usually fired in a layer on top of the tile so it does not go all through, but there are a much wider range of colours available and it is easier to match the colours.

Machine made mosaic panels are random colour selections of tiles laid out on a grid and faced with heavy paper. They are fixed to the wall paper side up, the paper is then stripped away and the tiles grouted.

Handmade patterns are made in the same basic way, but the designer works from painted artwork for complicated patterns or on a grid for simple geometric ones. The tiles are laid upside down, so the work is done back to front and in reverse. Irregular shapes must be cut by hand, which is time consuming and expensive.

OPPOSITE TOP LEFT *Working out a design on the computer.*

OPPOSITE CENTRE LEFT *Drawing up a piece of full scale artwork, using a grid. One square represents one tile.*

OPPOSITE RIGHT *Transforming an abstract painting into squares so it can be used as a mosaic design.*

LEFT *Laying out the separate sheets of a design to check the pattern and colour matching.*

BOTTOM LEFT *Laying marble mosaic on the full size artwork, which also acts as the facing sheet. The tiles are laid upside down and glued into position so the design is viewed in reverse and from the back until it is installed. It is fixed with the paper facing sheet outwards, the paper is then stripped off and the tiles grouted.*

BOTTOM CENTRE *Cutting marble mosaic tiles by hand from a strip of marble.*

BELOW *Installing a mosaic cladding to the exterior of a dome.*

BOTTOM RIGHT *Detail of part of a dome mosaic design.*

STAINED GLASS

Stained glass is an ancient craft - churches with their exuberant rose windows and panels of religious scenes often date back to medieval times. These days there is an even wider range of colours and textures available as well as a variety of different types of glass for different applications.

The inherent beauty of the material will not be fully appreciated unless light is shining through it. Because of this requirement, as well as its delicate nature, stained glass has often been set high up, in high windows, skylights, domes.

Designs do not have to be formal geometric shapes, although these can be very effective and the material is easily cut into such shapes. More organic design forms can be achieved by a variety of methods and modern technology also offers much more subtlety in shade and colour.

OPPOSITE *Freeform stained glass skylight over an informal double height entrance hall. The design depicts flowers and foliage round the edge, the green of the foliage gradually becoming shades of blue in the 'sky'.*

BELOW *Design for a triple window in a more formal and traditional style.*

OPPOSITE *Skylight panel above the staircase leading out of an entrance hall. Here the geometric design has a Mondrian feel, but the effect is softened with the introduction of filigree decorated frosted panels at intervals.*

LEFT *The windows behind the main seating area in the entrance hall also have a strong geometric pattern.*

BELOW *View across the entrance hall showing the stained glass panels in windows and doors. The stained glass adds richness and colour to the area.*

LEFT *Triple windows set high above the floor, beneath a dome. The rich colours of the stained glass are echoed in the painted plasterwork.*

BELOW *Alternative initial designs for the triple windows.*

BOTTOM *View of the whole dome. The geometric patterns in the plasterwork relate to those in the stained glass.*

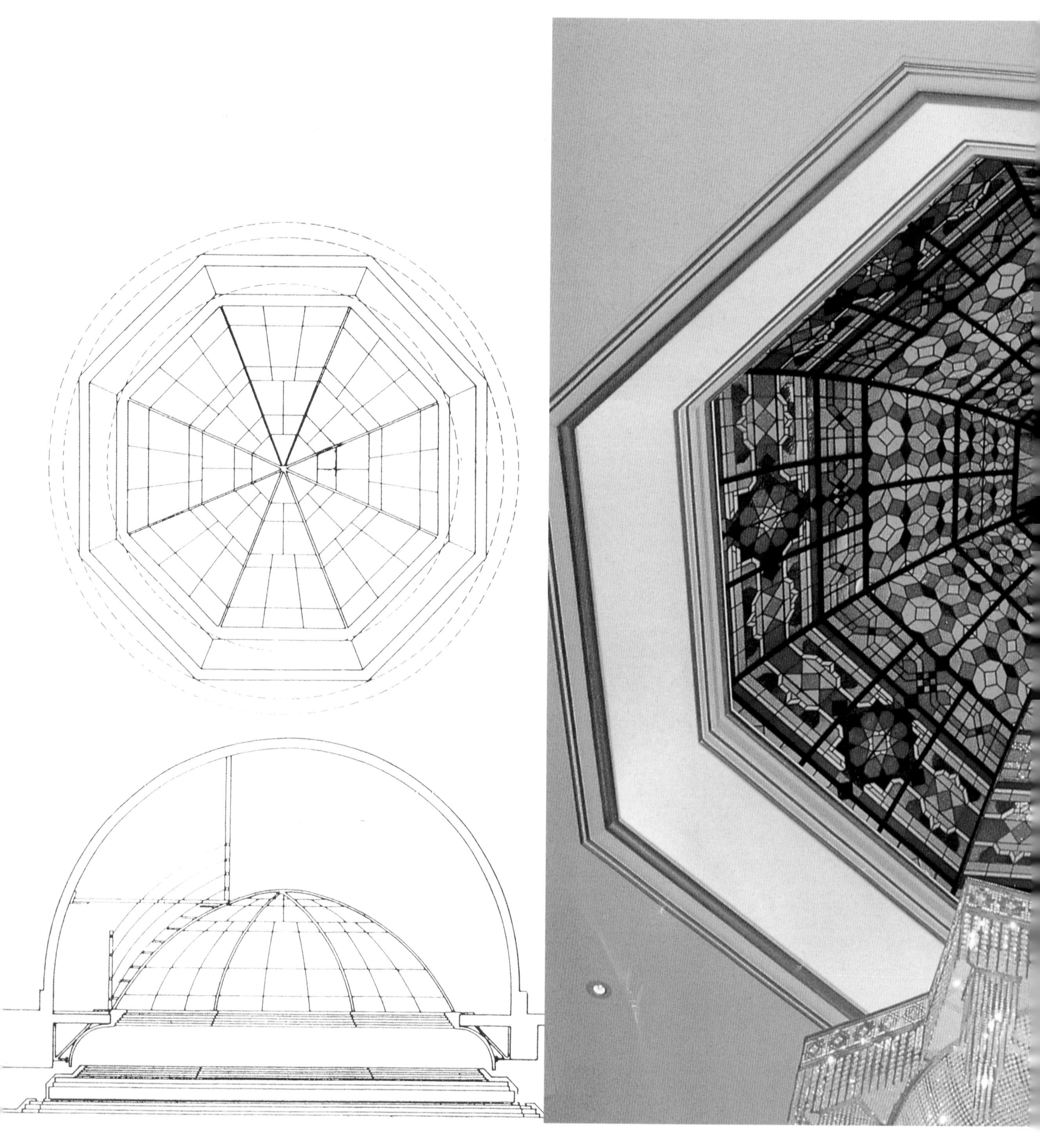

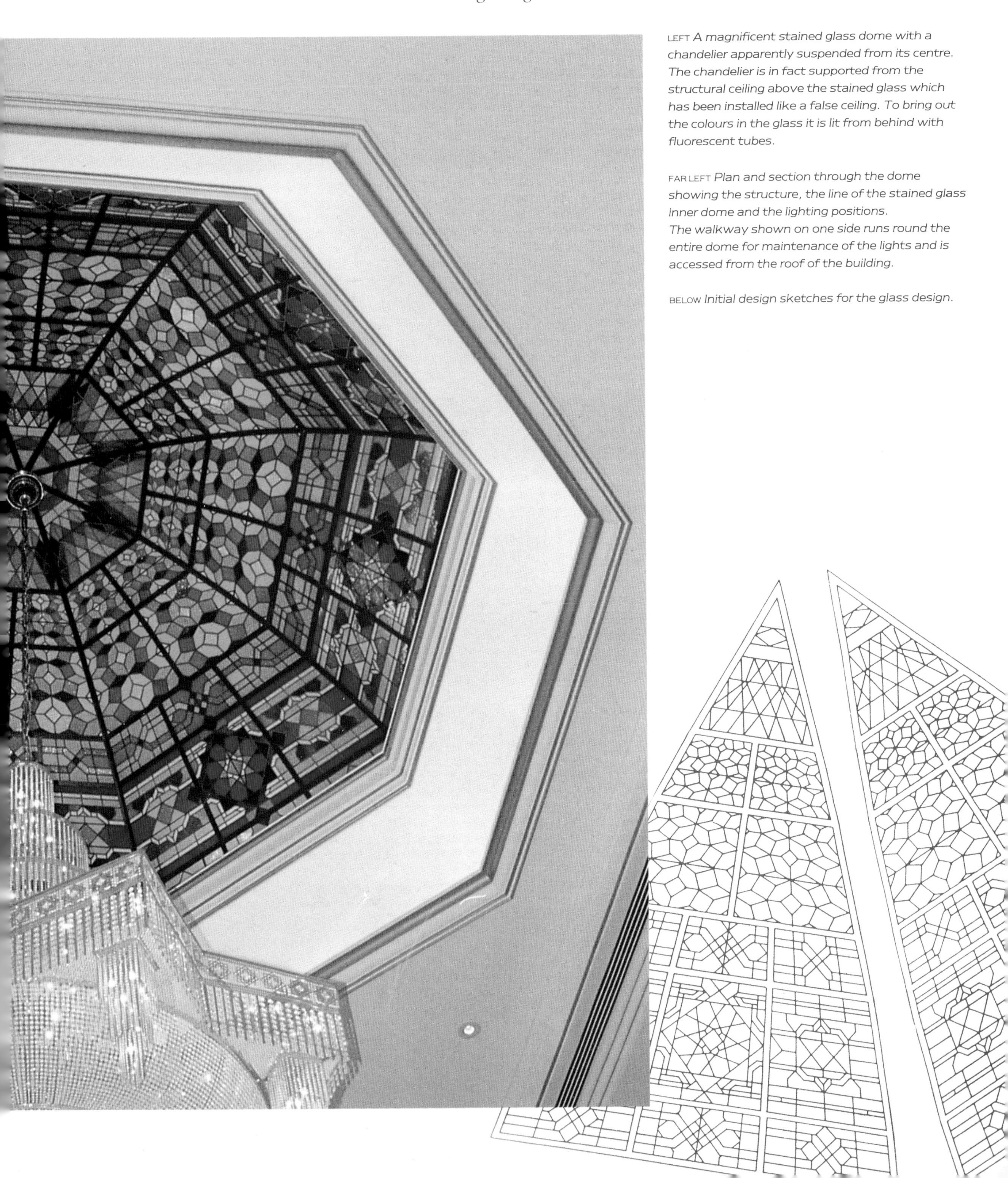

LEFT *A magnificent stained glass dome with a chandelier apparently suspended from its centre. The chandelier is in fact supported from the structural ceiling above the stained glass which has been installed like a false ceiling. To bring out the colours in the glass it is lit from behind with fluorescent tubes.*

FAR LEFT *Plan and section through the dome showing the structure, the line of the stained glass inner dome and the lighting positions. The walkway shown on one side runs round the entire dome for maintenance of the lights and is accessed from the roof of the building.*

BELOW *Initial design sketches for the glass design.*

BELOW *Simple square skylight above a stairwell, with geometric design stained glass.*

BOTTOM *Circular stained glass panel around a chandelier which hangs down a stairwell. A small skylight above lets light through the stained glass. The Art Deco feel to the design is a theme which has been carried through from the window and door panels in the entrance hall beneath.*

RIGHT *Circular skylight above an entrance hall with an elaborate and formal geometric design.*

OPPOSITE TOP *Stained glass central section to a glass roof over a swimming pool. The freeform shape of the plants gives a very informal feel to the design, while the panels in shades of blue suggest a sunny sky.*

OPPOSITE BOTTOM *Detail of part of the design.*

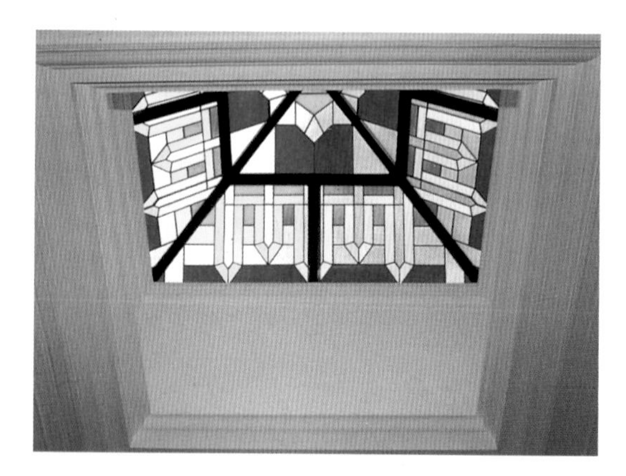

OPPOSITE *Entrance doors to a mosque designed with traditional geometric pierced work, filled with stained glass. Only two colours of glass are used, but the design is still very rich because of the glowing colours of the glass.*

BELOW *Floor length window in a coordinating design in the side wall of the mosque.*

BELOW LEFT *Detail of the stained glass design from the window.*

BOTTOM *View across the mosque. The stained glass throws a rich coloured light across the area, more than compensating for the very plain design of the walls and floor.*

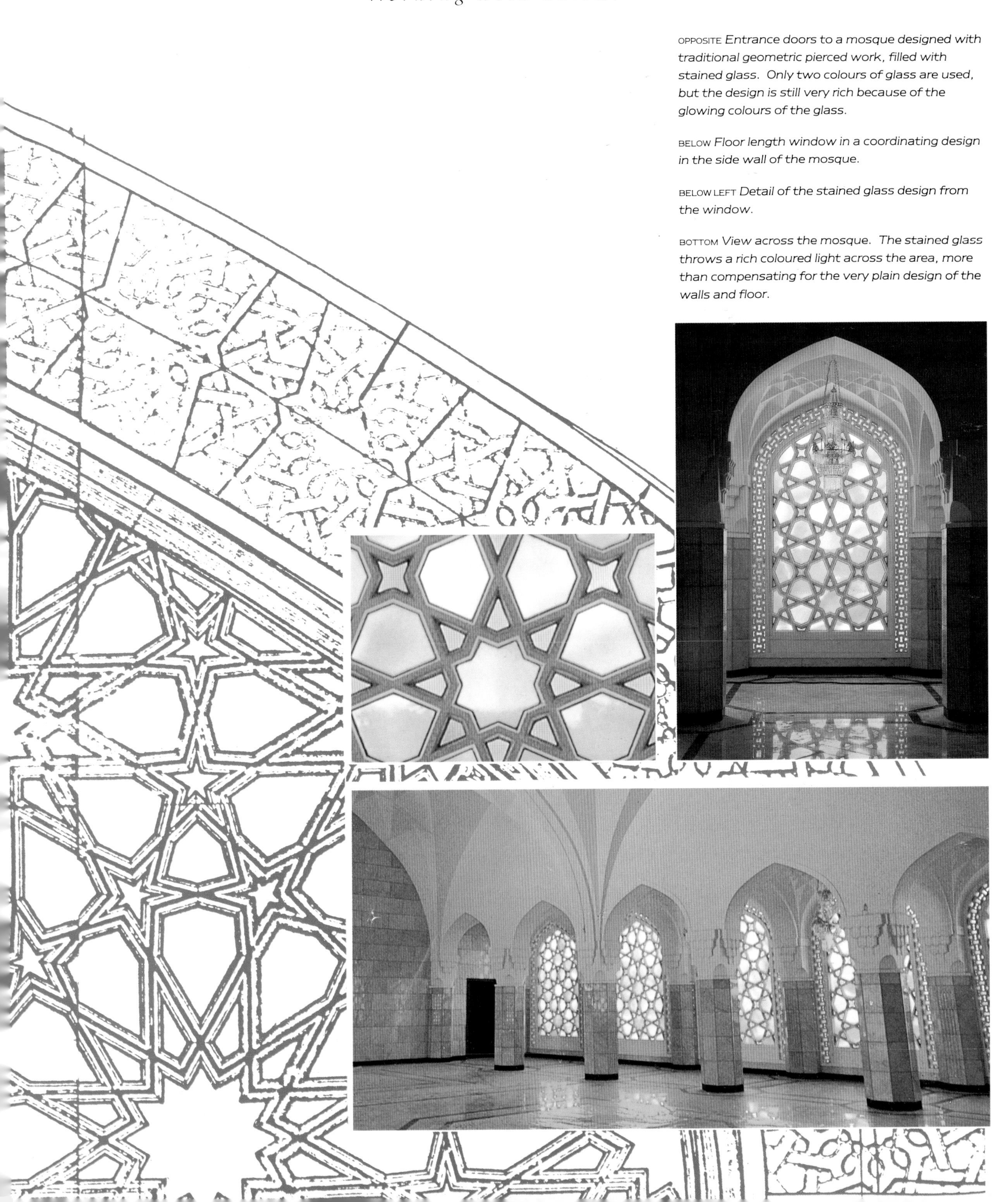

C.E.
K
CLEAN
1989

STAINED GLASS
Understanding the Techniques

Stained glass windows admit light, while at the same time varying its intensity and adding pattern and colour. The basic requirement for a successful stained glass installation is adequate light, whether this is natural or artificial.

Designs are made up of individual pieces of glass set into some kind of solid framework, usually made of strips of soft lead. Each piece of glass will therefore have a dark outline and this must be taken into account in the design.

Once the stained glass panel has been designed and the colours selected, the outline of the design must be drawn up to full scale to be used as a template for cutting the glass shapes and forming the framework. Working on a light box to judge the effect, each piece of glass is cut to fit its allotted space and fixed into position with the lead framing. When the panel is finished the lead strips are burnished firmly into place and the panel is ready to be installed.

OPPOSITE *Drawing up the outlines of the design at full scale. This is known as a cartoon.*

TOP LEFT *Laying a piece of coloured glass over the cartoon on a light box to add painted details to the design.*

TOP RIGHT *Placing the pieces of glass in the design and fixing them in position with lead strips, known as cames.*

CENTRE LEFT *Tapping the lead cames into place.*

CENTRE RIGHT *Brushing putty into the lead cames, so the pieces of glass are held firmly in place.*

BOTTOM *Checking the colours against a light source.*

METALWORK

Decorative metalwork comes in many shapes, forms and designs and in many materials. The most commonly used metals are iron - as in wrought ironwork - brass and bronze, as well as various alloys.

There are very few limitations when designing in metal, the raw material is relatively simple to work. It can be cast, formed or welded into shape, so complex shapes and designs can be achieved very easily. A variety of decorative finishes can also be applied to most metals to protect or add colour or texture, while brass and bronze can also be polished. Finishes are generally very durable, even when used on the exterior of buildings.

Metal is often used because of its strength, but there is no reason why it should not be a decorative feature at the same time. Exposed external framing to buildings can be both decorative and structural, as can the balusters in a staircase. The most extensive use of decorative metalwork is for fences and grilles, which are not only used to decorate the exterior of a building but also to add a measure of security.

OPPOSITE *Decorative metalwork fence around the edge of a building. The shapes in the metal echo the architectural features of the wall behind.*

BELOW *Gold filigree work.*

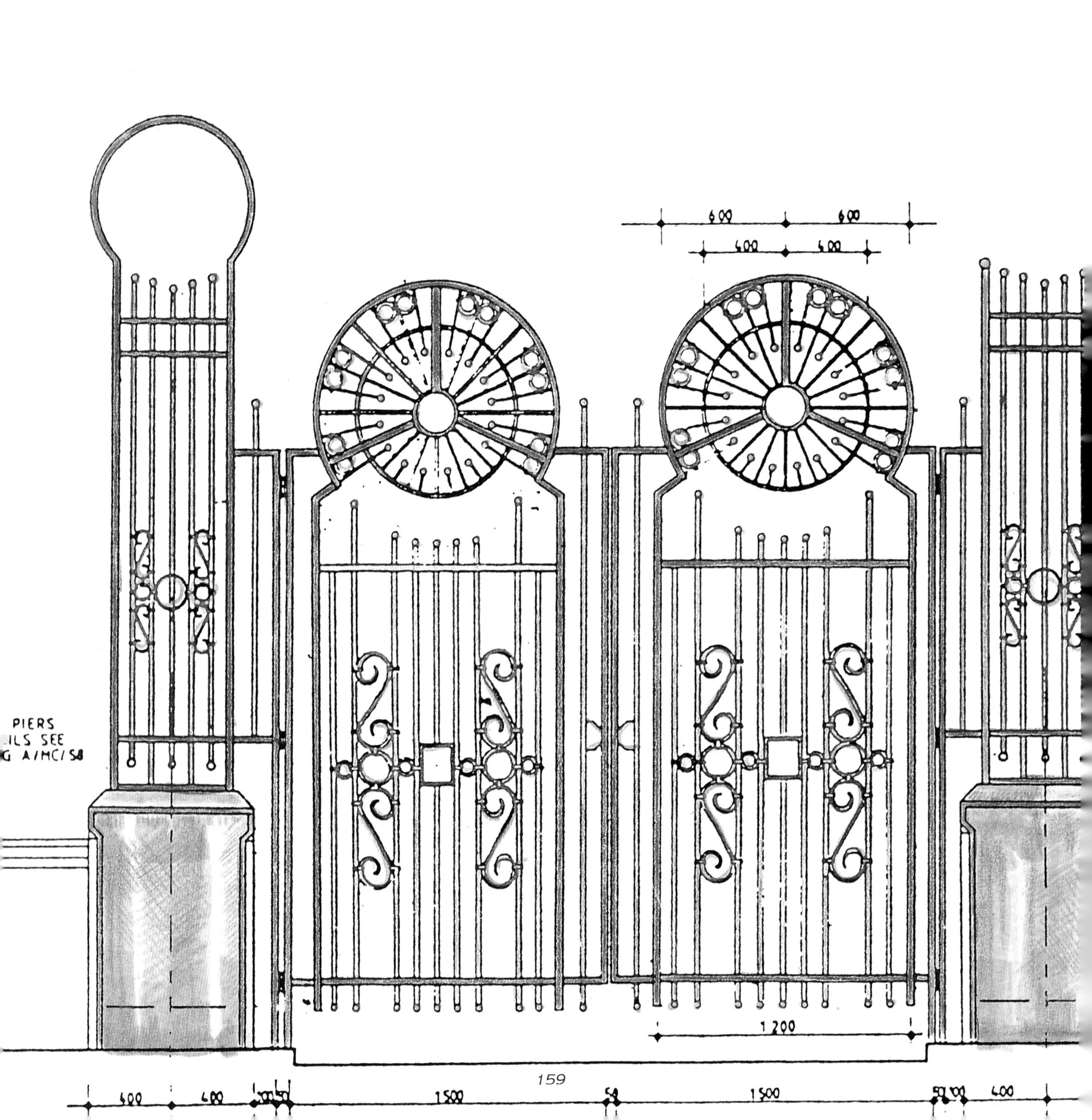
600
600
400
400
PIERS
ILS SEE
G A/MC/S8
1 200
400
400
1500
50
1500
400

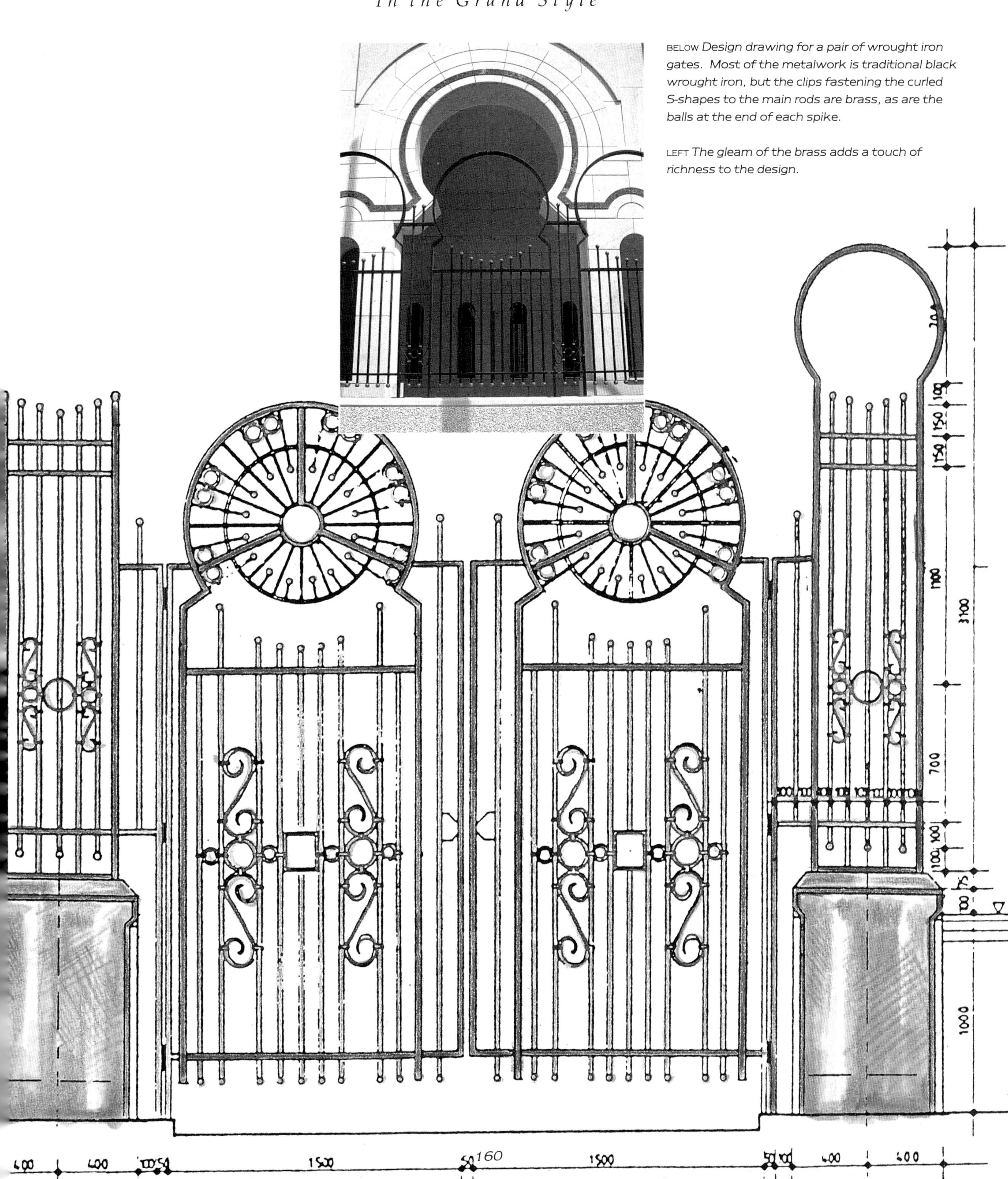

BELOW *Design drawing for a pair of wrought iron gates. Most of the metalwork is traditional black wrought iron, but the clips fastening the curled S-shapes to the main rods are brass, as are the balls at the end of each spike.*

LEFT *The gleam of the brass adds a touch of richness to the design.*

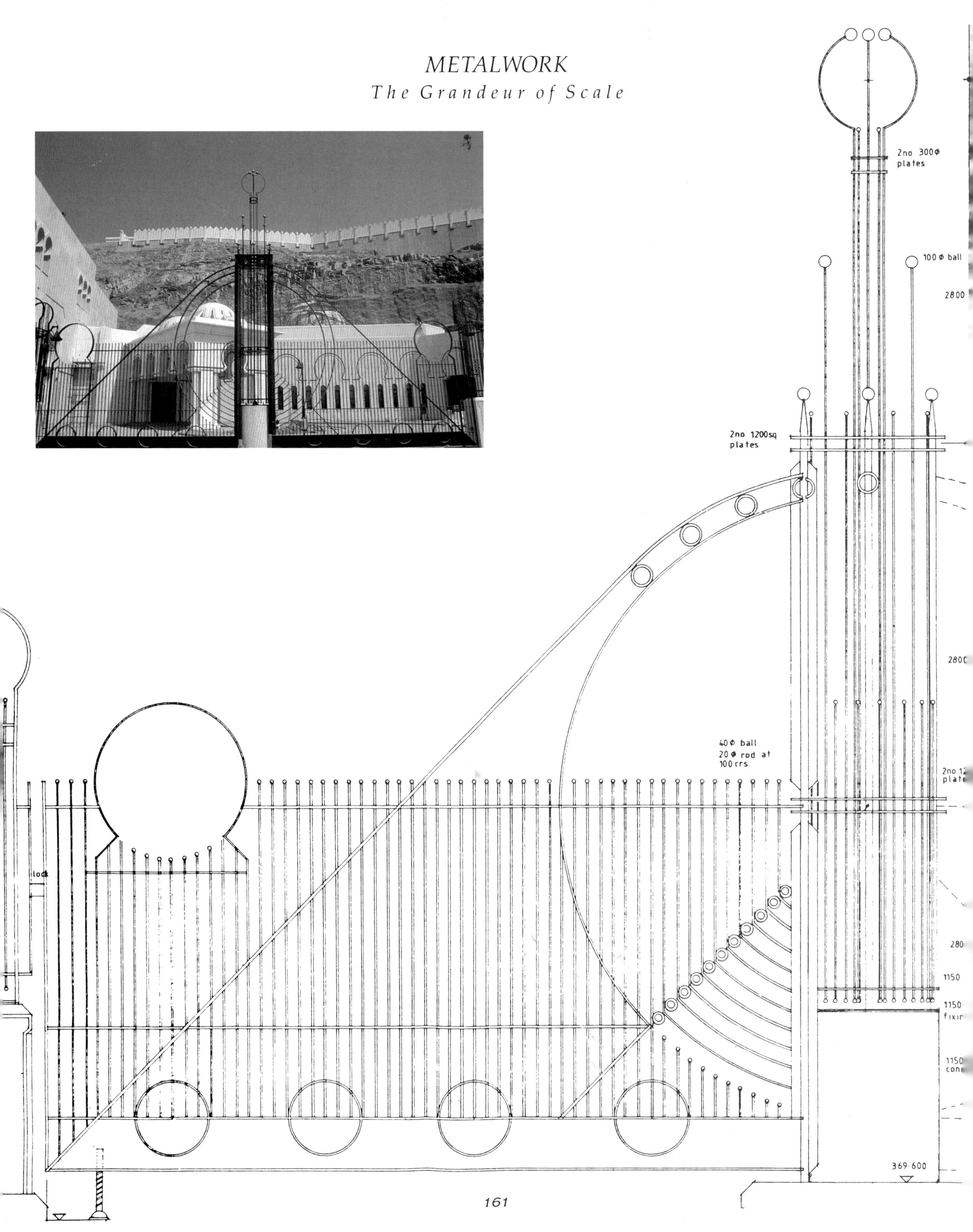
2no 300φ
plates
100 φ ball
2800
2no 1200sq
plates
2800
40 φ ball
20 φ rod at
100 crs.
2800
1150
1150
1150
369.600

OPPOSITE *Main ceremonial gate in to a large public building. The massive centre circle reflects the circular motif used in the architecture behind, while the central post adds a strong focal point. The gate is made in metal rod and decorated with brass balls.*

LEFT *Detail of the central post.*

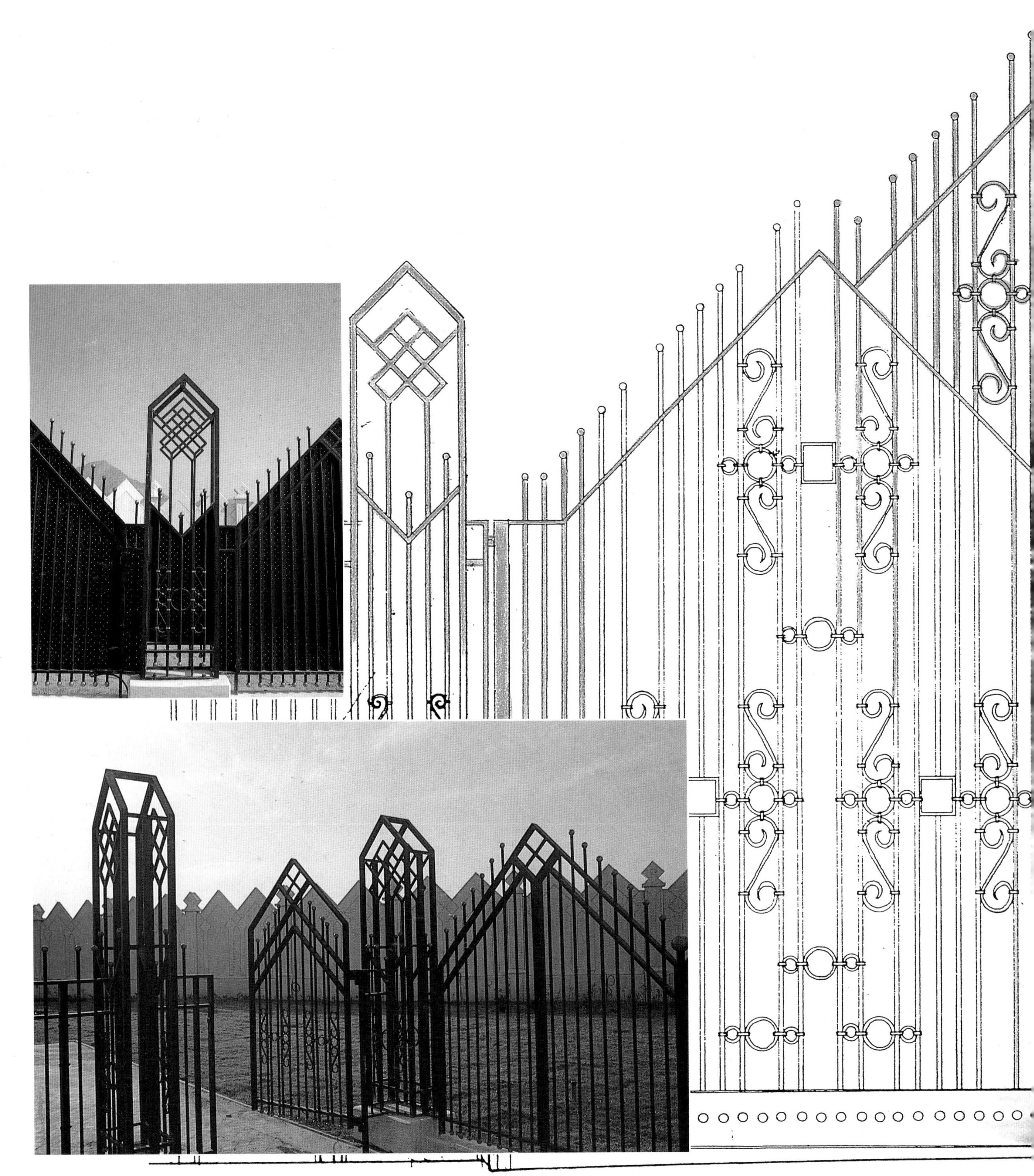

BELOW *Design drawing for a pair of wrought iron gates, using a similar theme as before, but without the circular motif.*

OPPOSITE TOP *Section of the fence near the gates where the design has been adapted to block the view of the building inside. A perforated metal panel has been shaped and fixed behind the rods of the fence. The pattern of the holes makes the panel appear lighter in relation to the fence than if it had been a solid sheet.*

OPPOSITE BOTTOM *Small access gate and section of the fence without the metal panels. In the background a prefabricated concrete wall on the edge of a cliff echoes the shapes in the fence.*

METALWORK
Creating a Theme

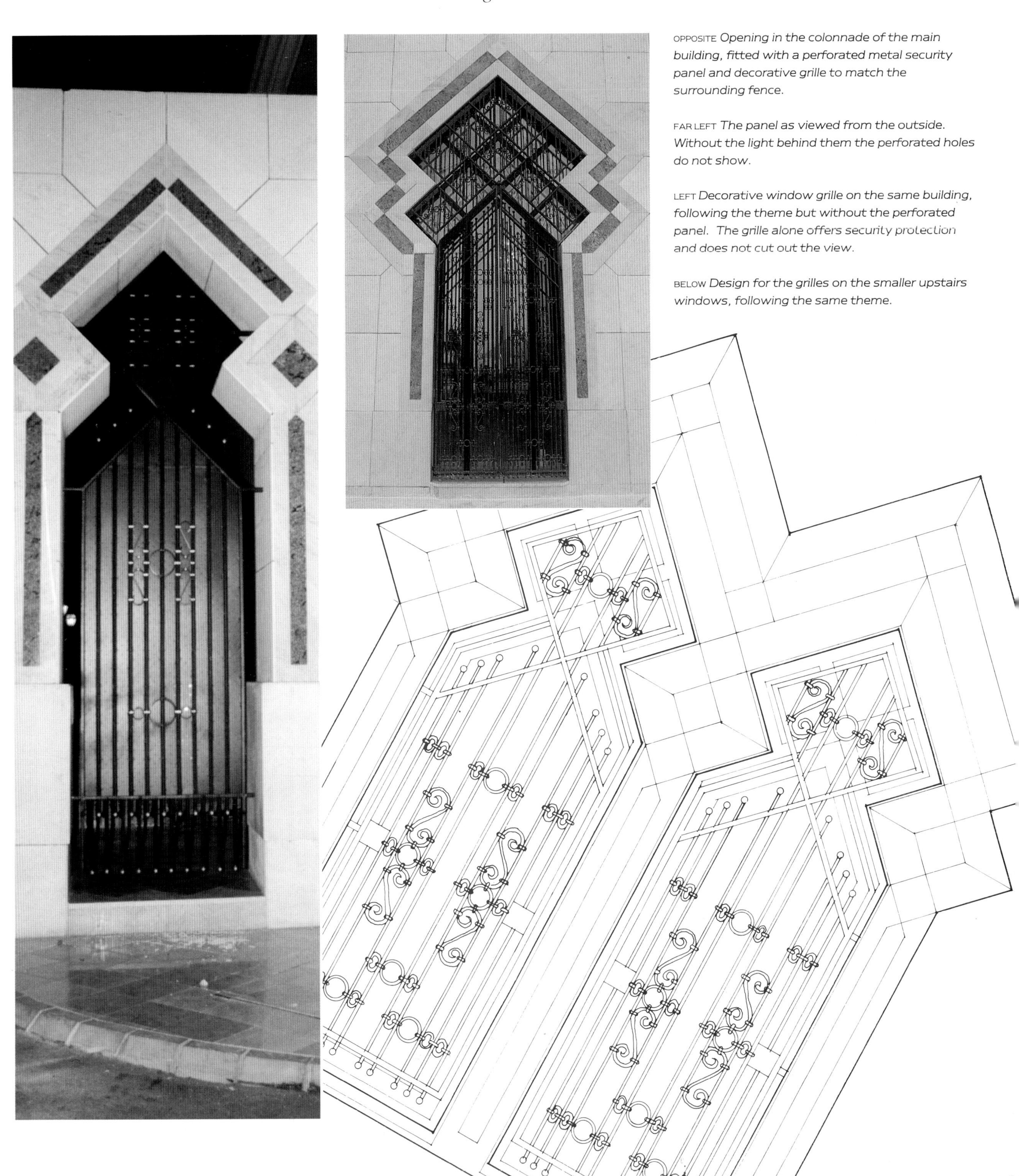

OPPOSITE *Opening in the colonnade of the main building, fitted with a perforated metal security panel and decorative grille to match the surrounding fence.*

FAR LEFT *The panel as viewed from the outside. Without the light behind them the perforated holes do not show.*

LEFT *Decorative window grille on the same building, following the theme but without the perforated panel. The grille alone offers security protection and does not cut out the view.*

BELOW *Design for the grilles on the smaller upstairs windows, following the same theme.*

METALWORK

Attention to Details

OPPOSITE TOP *Design drawing for a fence using concrete pillars with iron rod fencework between them, featuring cast brass geometric panels.*

OPPOSITE CENTRE *Detail of cast brass panel.*

OPPOSITE BOTTOM *Each column has a carriage light, with a framework in cast brass, mounted on a level with the decorative brass panel.*

LEFT *Design drawing for the carriage light and a matching lamp post.*

BELOW *Prototype for the cast brass framework of the light.*

OPPOSITE *Decorative staircase panels in a geometric design, in keeping with the Art Deco feel to the rest of the area. The main framework is hammered steel, with brass detailing.*

LEFT *The central part of this first floor room is open through to the ground floor, to create a double height area in the centre of the reception hall beneath. The railings around the opening are designed on a formal repeating motif, in keeping with the formal air of the rest of the space.*

BELOW LEFT *Again these are railings around a central floor opening, but in a much less formal space. The design of the railings is much more freeform and lighter in style.*

BELOW *This staircase rising out of a fairly plain entrance hall is the main focal point of the area. The complex design of the staircase adds a touch of richness and elegance.*

OPPOSITE LEFT *A footbridge across a busy main road in a Middle Eastern city, detail of the top of one of the towers supporting the structure.*

OPPOSITE RIGHT *A spiral precast metal staircase leads up from street level.*

BOTTOM *Original design elevation for the footbridge, which is supported on three towers - one at each side of the street and one on the central reservation.*

LEFT *The sides of the footbridge are precast metal panels using a traditional geometric motif. Shading is needed because of the hot sun, and this is provided by tensioned canvas over each section.*

BELOW *Detail of one of the side panels.*

FAR LEFT *Footbridge across a busy main road, leading to a shopping centre. The shapes in the metal framework are highlighted with a bright yellow enamel finish, which also protects the metal from corrosion.*

LEFT *Four towers mark where the footbridge links into the building. The same yellow enamelled geometric framework runs up the sides of the towers, to form a cluster of openwork spires, each tipped with a glass globe. At night the globes are illuminated and the spires are outlined with fluorescent light.*

BOTTOM *Inside the ceiling is open, exposing the framework above.*

LIGHTING

Any enclosed space will need some form of artificial lighting if it is to be used during the hours of darkness, but there are also hundreds of ways in which light can be used to change the mood of an area and to add interesting special effects.

Decorative light fittings basically divide into two groups - those that are decorative within themselves and are used visually as a feature in the room, and those which are unobtrusive but which provide special lighting effects. Sometimes these two functions are combined in one fitting, but it is more usual to combine the two different types of light fitting in one area to achieve the desired effect. Chandeliers are the ultimate example of a decorative light fitting but are often thought of as only being in the classical style, although in fact they come in a variety of designs including very modern styles.

Lighting can be dramatic or subtle, throw a strong white beam in a particular direction, or glow with soft diffuse colours. Whatever effect is desired there is a light fitting designed to achieve it.

OPPOSITE *A row of specially designed three metre high classic style crystal chandeliers in a grand entrance hall. The smaller chandeliers on each side are a scaled down version of the same design.*

BELOW *Looking straight up at one of the large chandeliers, two metres in diameter.*

LIGHTING
In the Grand Style

LEFT *A massive formal state dining room with specially designed classic style crystal chandeliers. The pin spots in the ceiling not only add background light, but also highlight the crystals in the chandelier and make them sparkle even more.*

BELOW *Initial sketch design of the shape needed to fit into the decor of the room.*

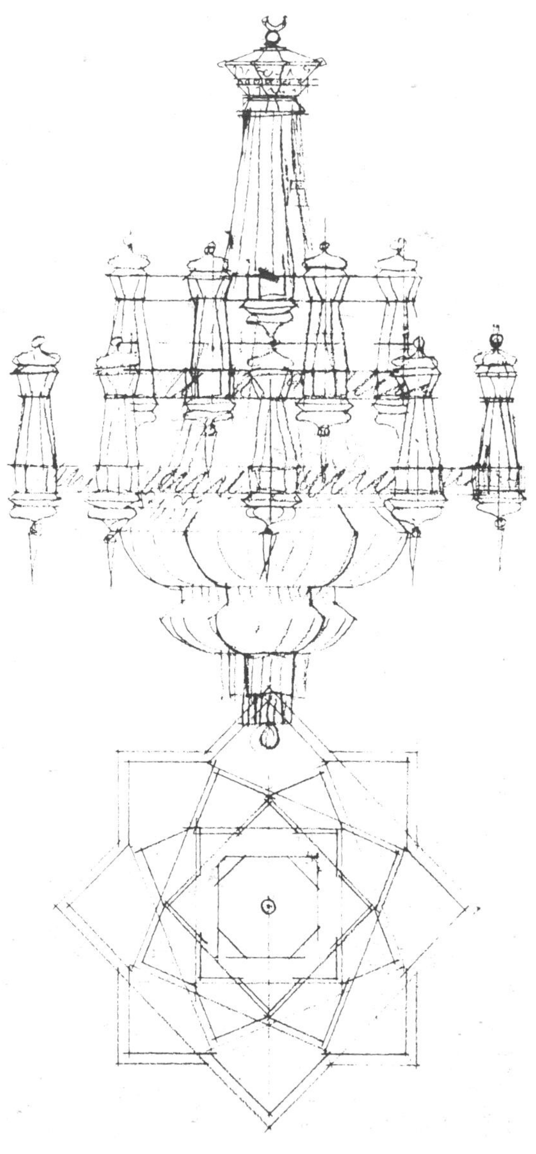

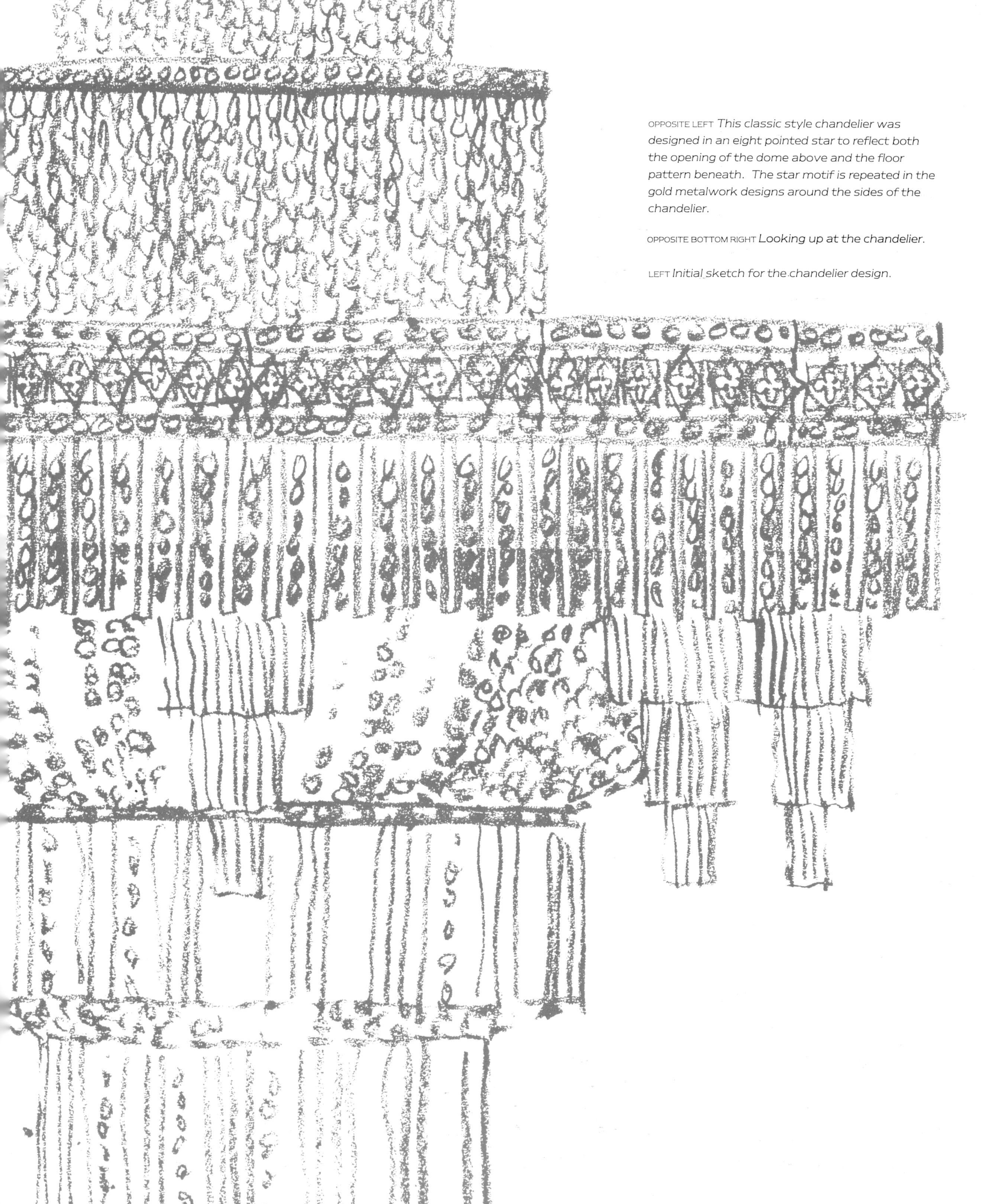

OPPOSITE LEFT *This classic style chandelier was designed in an eight pointed star to reflect both the opening of the dome above and the floor pattern beneath. The star motif is repeated in the gold metalwork designs around the sides of the chandelier.*

OPPOSITE BOTTOM RIGHT *Looking up at the chandelier.*

LEFT *Initial sketch for the chandelier design.*

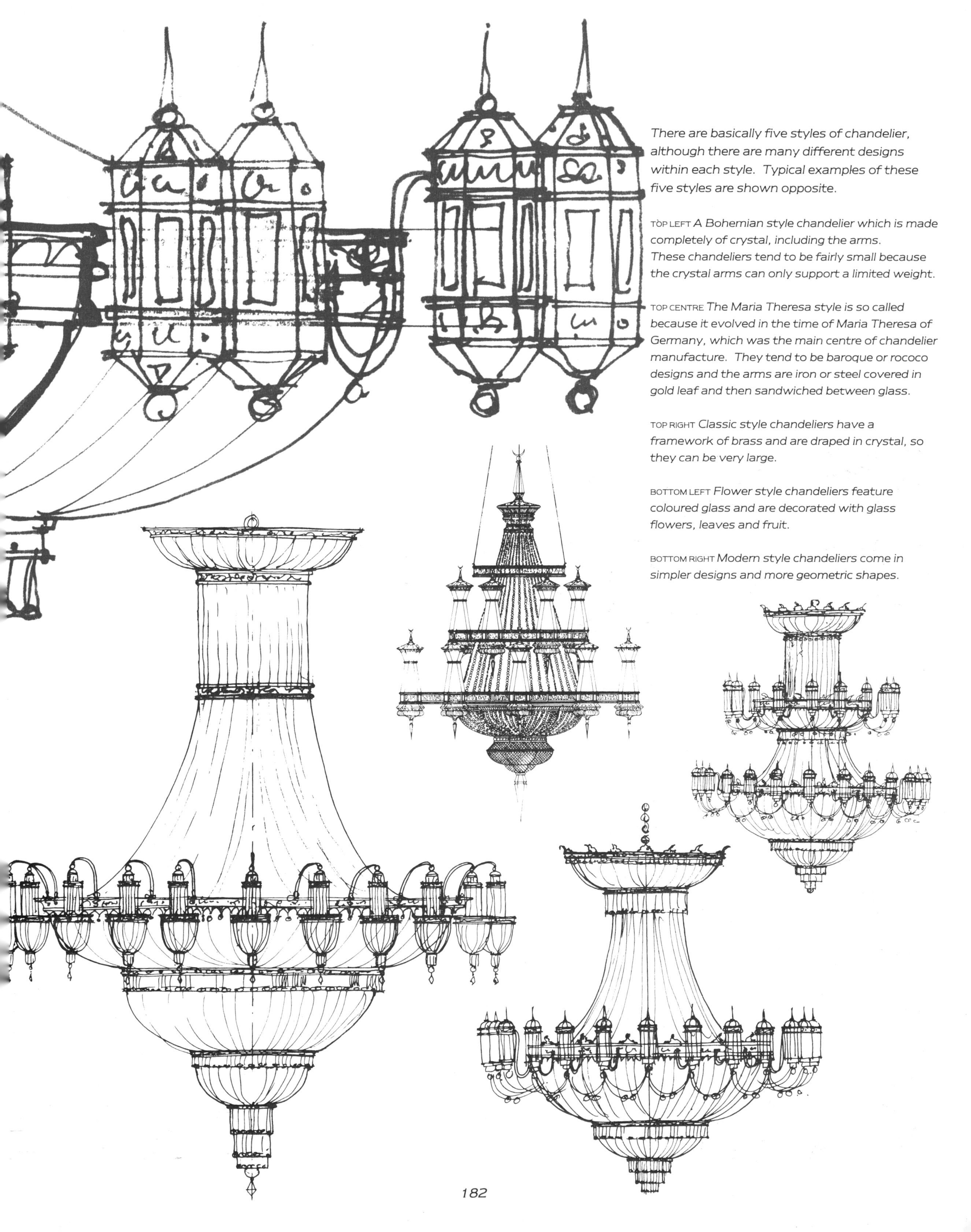

There are basically five styles of chandelier, although there are many different designs within each style. Typical examples of these five styles are shown opposite.

TOP LEFT *A Bohemian style chandelier which is made completely of crystal, including the arms. These chandeliers tend to be fairly small because the crystal arms can only support a limited weight.*

TOP CENTRE *The Maria Theresa style is so called because it evolved in the time of Maria Theresa of Germany, which was the main centre of chandelier manufacture. They tend to be baroque or rococo designs and the arms are iron or steel covered in gold leaf and then sandwiched between glass.*

TOP RIGHT *Classic style chandeliers have a framework of brass and are draped in crystal, so they can be very large.*

BOTTOM LEFT *Flower style chandeliers feature coloured glass and are decorated with glass flowers, leaves and fruit.*

BOTTOM RIGHT *Modern style chandeliers come in simpler designs and more geometric shapes.*

BELOW *Small wall lantern with ornate filigree work decoration.*

RIGHT *The wall lanterns in position in the bathroom, adding a touch of rich pattern to the relatively plain design.*

BELOW *In some areas chandeliers may not be appropriate although there is still a need for some kind of decorative light fitting. Here a decorative lantern and matching wall lantern have been designed for a corridor.*

LEFT *The wall lantern in situ in the corridor. The design for the area is based on strong, bold shapes and the lanterns fit in well with this theme.*

PLAN

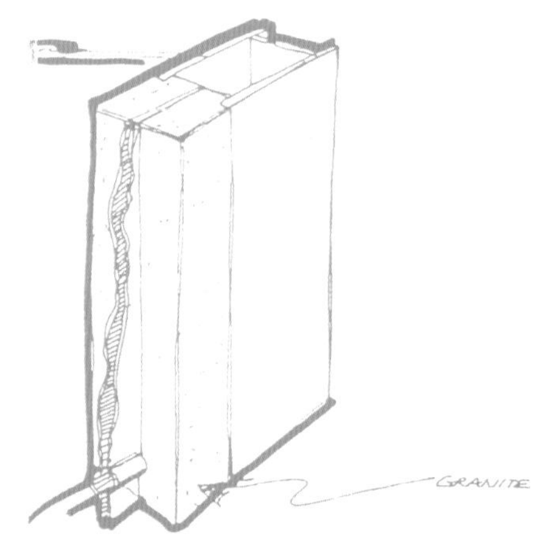

OPPOSITE *Design and prototype for a modern table lamp using granite and sandblasted glass.*

LEFT *Exterior waterproof lighting used to highlight a fountain.*

BELOW *Columns designed as an architectural feature but including uplights. Uplighting works best with a white ceiling to reflect the light and diffuse it across the room.*

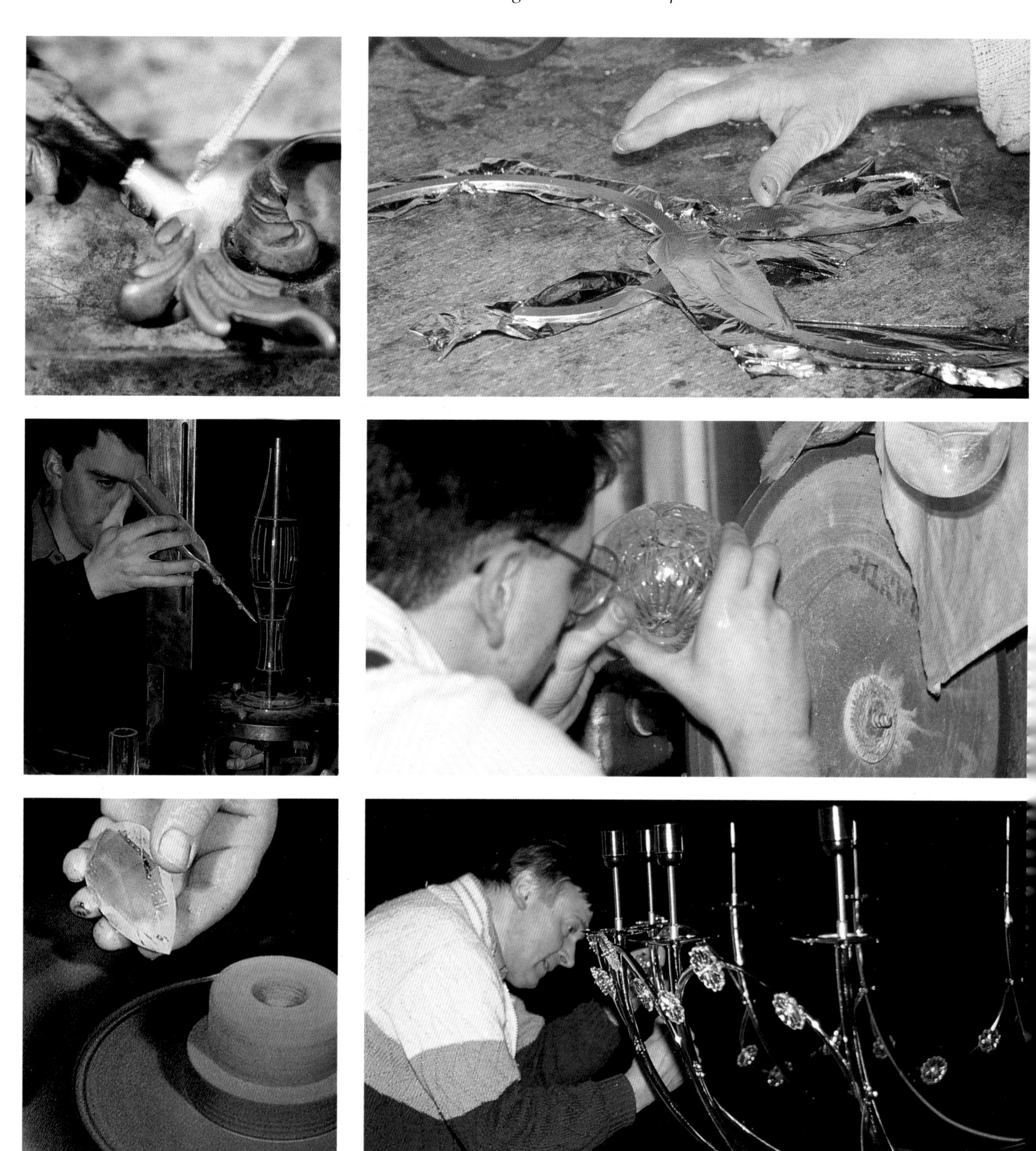

Understanding the Techniques

Many chandeliers are still made very much in the traditional way, particularly those in traditional styles. They consist of a framework, either of glass or metal, a light source and decorative glass or crystal drops to both conceal the direct light source from the eye and reflect the light from it across the room.

The frame of the chandelier sets its basic size and shape, but there are hundreds of different drops in all shapes and designs which can be added to the framework. The difference between crystal and glass drops is that the crystal reflects the light much better and so is brighter and more colourful. Most of the glass in a chandelier is hand cut, pressed or cast glass shapes do not reflect the light as well although they are used in some designs.

The chandelier is also assembled by hand, each drop or series of drops being hung individually from its own hook.

OPPOSITE TOP LEFT *Welding and forming the metal framework to a chandelier.*

OPPOSITE TOP RIGHT *Applying gold leaf to the flat metal framework of a Maria Theresa style chandelier before the decorative glass is added to each side.*

OPPOSITE CENTRE LEFT *Marking up the pattern on a glass before cutting.*

OPPOSITE CENTRE RIGHT *Hand cutting the design into the glass.*

OPPOSITE BOTTOM LEFT *Polishing the facets of a crystal drop by hand.*

OPPOSITE BOTTOM RIGHT *Hanging the crystal drops on the framework.*

RIGHT *Assembling and wiring the chandelier.*

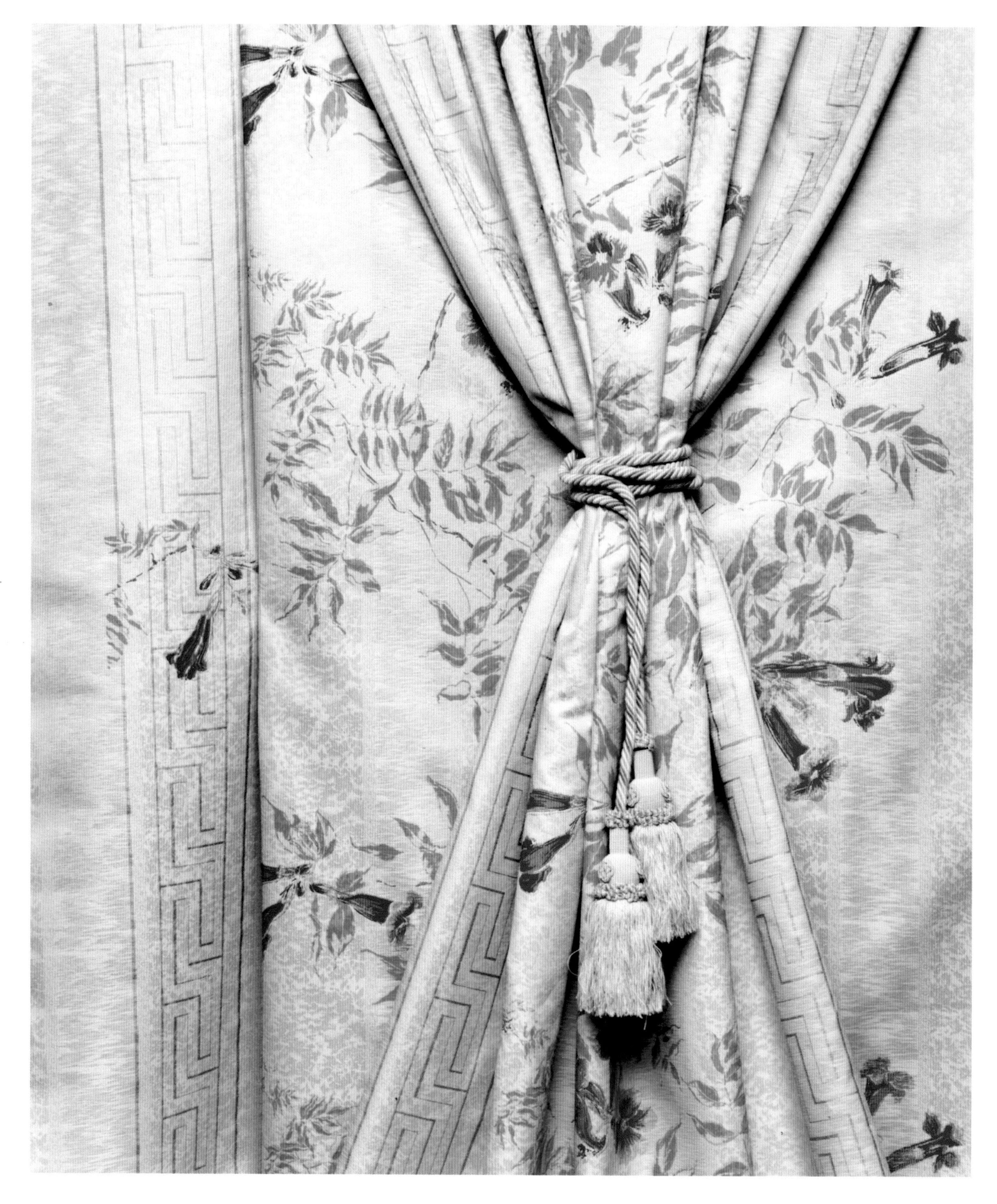

FABRICS

Fabric is a very versatile material that is often under-used. It comes in a variety of weights, from stiff and strong to a flimsy, gossamer veil, it can be woven plain or with a pattern, printed, painted, dyed or embroidered and can be stretched or sewn into quite complex shapes. The colour can be changed easily to suit any colour scheme, it can be woven in a variety of widths and almost any length.

As well as the wide range of standard fabrics that are available, many manufacturers also offer designs which are specially printed to match the rest of the colour scheme. Fabric designs can also be commissioned, which guarantees that the design will be unique.

Fabric can be used on walls or ceilings to add a feeling of luxury and this will also help to cut down noise levels in large open areas. Fabric for this type of use can be paperbacked, stretched, padded round panels or pleated, each of which will give a different overall effect to the room.

OPPOSITE *A specially designed fabric for a dining room. The pattern weave of the base fabric creates a textured background which was then over printed with the design in seven colours.*

BELOW *The finished fabric made up into curtains.*

FABRICS
Creating a Theme

LEFT *This large dining room has specially designed curtain fabric, upholstery fabric and carpet, in colours to coordinate with the marble in the room. The base colour used throughout is a pale green, picked up from the light veining in the marble.*

OPPOSITE *The striped curtain fabric, with matching colours for the fringe and tie backs, and the upholstery fabric, woven in green with a gold design.*

OPPOSITE BOTTOM RIGHT *The carpet design, with background colour matching the upholstery and main curtain colour. The seven colours used in the border design match those in the curtain fabric.*

BELOW *The windows are nearly six metres high, so an extra long fringe was needed.*

FABRICS
In the Grand Style

OPPOSITE *Curtain fabric with bold bright design for a large sitting room with very high windows.*

LEFT *The final artwork for the main fabric and border, with alternative colouring of the geometric grid. The lighter version was chosen so the curtains would not look too heavy.*

CENTRE LEFT *The original sketch design, picking up colours from other fabrics in the room.*

BOTTOM LEFT *The carpet design uses a similar motif and the same colours.*

BELOW *When the fabric is made up into curtains, the geometric motif is carefully placed so it is symmetrical within the curtain design.*

RIGHT *Curtains in a specially designed fabric. The gold in the design catches the light and looks very rich.*

BELOW *The original sketch design, using colours and motifs from the other fabrics in the room, and the finished artwork.*

BOTTOM *Detail of the finished fabric. The cream background fabric already has a woven design and this is overprinted with the floral motif. The pink is added to the petals by hand painting each one.*

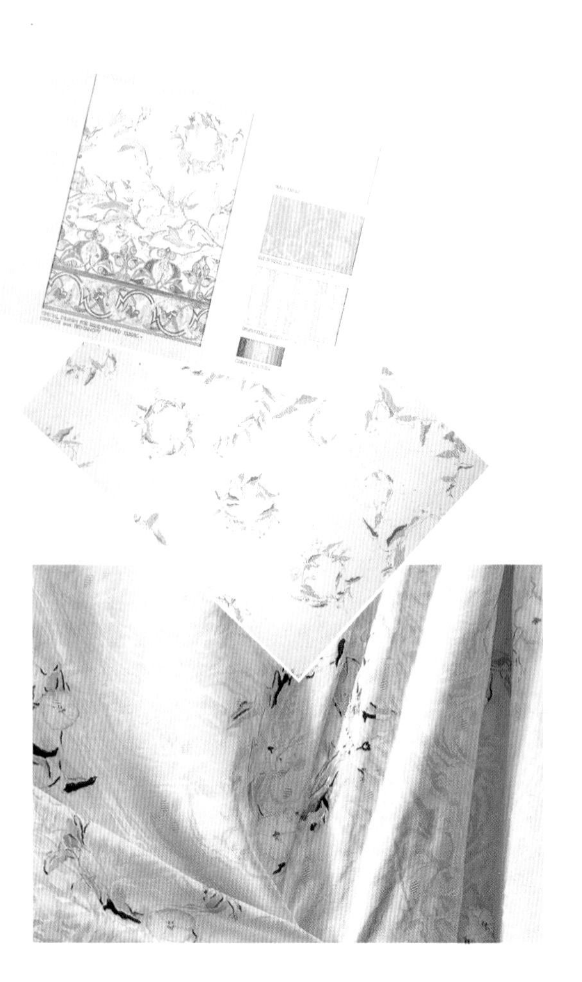

LEFT *Many of the bedroom colours are carried through to the sitting room, which is part of the same suite. Detail of the fabric design for this room.*

BELOW *The original fabric design for the sitting room, with the other fabrics in the room.*

BOTTOM *The finished fabric made up into curtains.*

The basic formal curtain design, using swags and tails, can be adapted to give a variety of different looks.

RIGHT *Asymmetrical designs can be very dramatic.*

CENTRE *Double tails make the basic design look more ornate.*

FAR RIGHT CENTRE *Contrast lining to the tails can be very effective.*

FAR RIGHT BOTTOM *Contrast swags and tails add extra colour to the window area, balancing the darker colours used elsewhere in the room.*

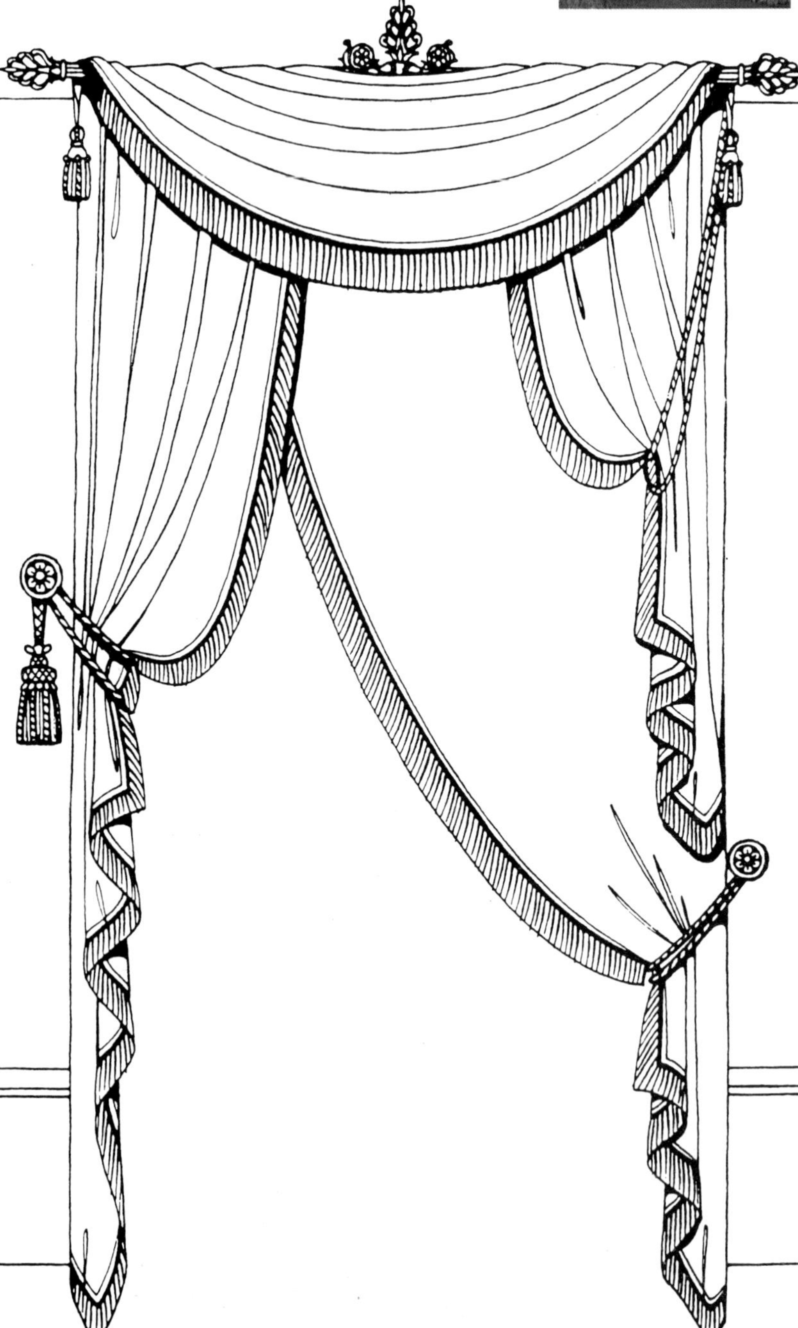

Fabric is an easy material to work with and can quickly be transformed. Dyeing plain fabric is a very simple method of customising it, and if it has a woven design this can often be accentuated as the different textures take up the colour in different amounts.
Most fabric can also be easily printed with a unique design. Once the pattern has been designed, it is drawn up at full scale and coloured as a guide for making the screens. Each area of colour is blocked in on a separate transparent cell, which must register with the main design to ensure the colours will be printed in the right place. These cells are used to transfer the design photographically to the screens, one for each colour to be printed.
Extra details can be added by hand later; hand painting to highlight special areas, sewing on sequins or beads, embroidering areas to add texture.

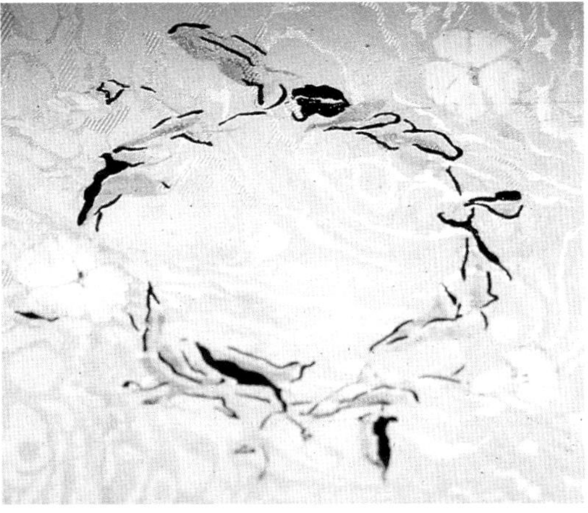

OPPOSITE *Hand painting the flower details on a length of printed fabric.*

TOP LEFT *Detail of the flower motif. The pink edging to the petals has been added by hand.*

TOP RIGHT *Checking the registration on the cells against the master design before the screens are made.*

CENTRE LEFT *Screen printing the fabric. The base material has been stretched and taped to the bench so it will not move during printing.*

CENTRE RIGHT *Alternative colourways can look very different.*

BELOW *Detail of a finished design.*

BOTTOM RIGHT *Checking the printed fabric against the artwork.*

CARPETS

Although the carpet often only functions as the backdrop to an interior design scheme, it can add a decorative impact of its own. Even machine made carpets now come in a variety of patterns, colours and textures, some with their own coordinating borders which can be cut into the body of the carpet when it is laid to make it look custom designed.

An individually designed hand made carpet will add even more to the atmosphere of a room. As well as matching the colours of the fabrics in the room, the design can pick up other motifs in the interior design scheme and be laid out to follow the shape of the room exactly.

There is a distinct difference between hand knotted and hand tufted carpets. In hand knotted carpets the lengths of wool or silk forming the pile are tied individually by hand, a very skilled and time consuming process which makes the carpet extremely expensive.

Hand tufted carpets are made by inserting the pile into a backing cloth using a hand held gun, which is considerably faster. This means that the carpet design can be totally individual, with colours matched to the interior design scheme, within a reasonable cost.

OPPOSITE *Handmade carpet in a formal salon in shades of blue and gold, colours which pick up the upholstery and wall fabrics.*

BELOW *Detail of part of the border design.*

CARPETS

Defining Areas

With a handmade carpet the borders and motifs of the design can be placed where they make the most effective impact; borders can echo the shape of the room.

BELOW RIGHT *Artwork, showing the placement of colours, with some of the sample tufts which the manufacturer will match to.*

OPPOSITE *The finished carpet in situ.*

OPPOSITE *Artwork for the central motif and border of a large formal salon carpet, showing the colour placement, with sample tufts for the manufacturer to match to. The central motif adds interest and colour to the centre of the room, which would otherwise be a plain area.*

OPPOSITE BOTTOM *Detail of the finished border design.*

LEFT *Formal salon carpet with border design, placed to fall in front of the furniture, and central motif.*

BELOW LEFT *Detail of border design.*

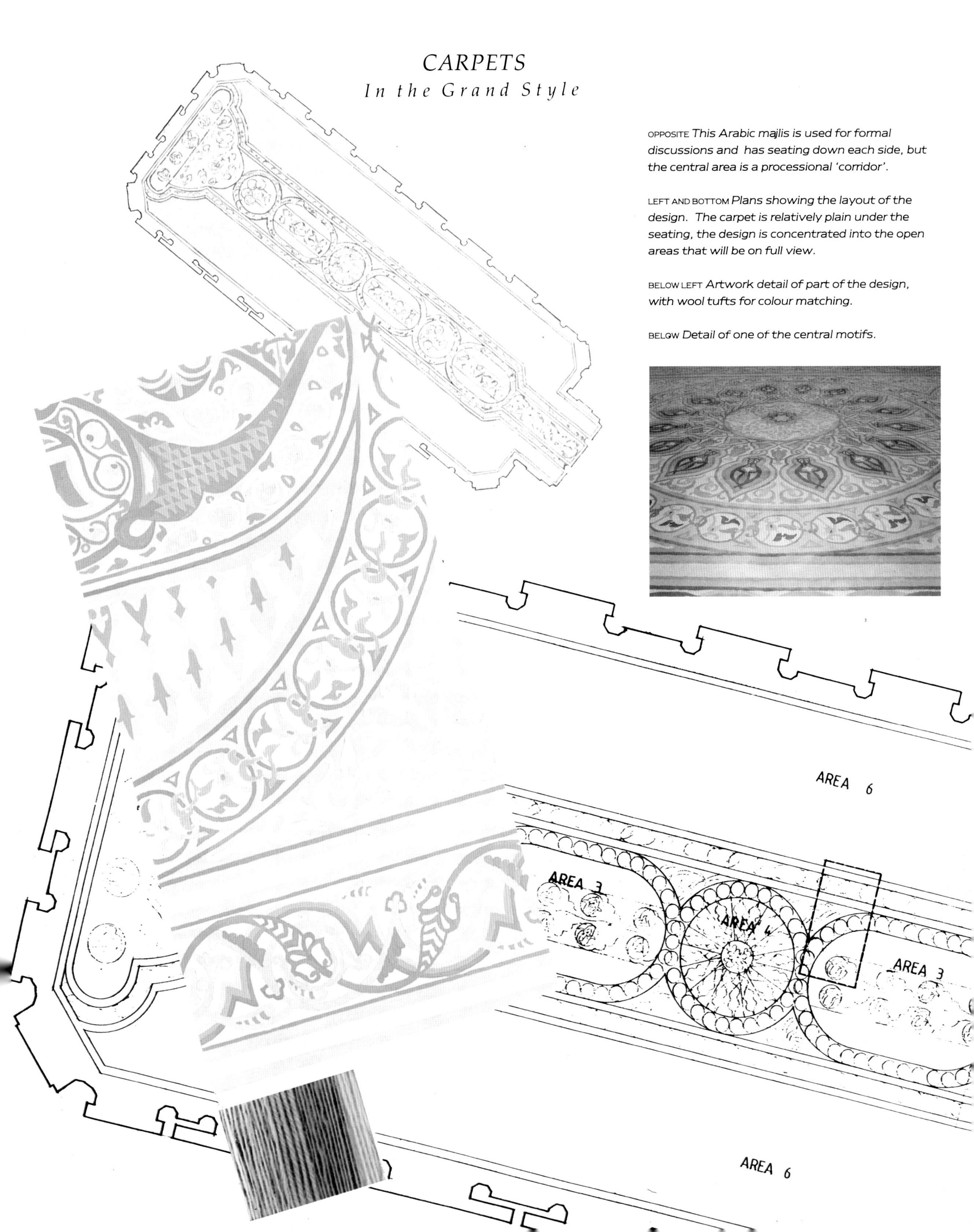

OPPOSITE *This Arabic majlis is used for formal discussions and has seating down each side, but the central area is a processional 'corridor'.*

LEFT AND BOTTOM *Plans showing the layout of the design. The carpet is relatively plain under the seating, the design is concentrated into the open areas that will be on full view.*

BELOW LEFT *Artwork detail of part of the design, with wool tufts for colour matching.*

BELOW *Detail of one of the central motifs.*

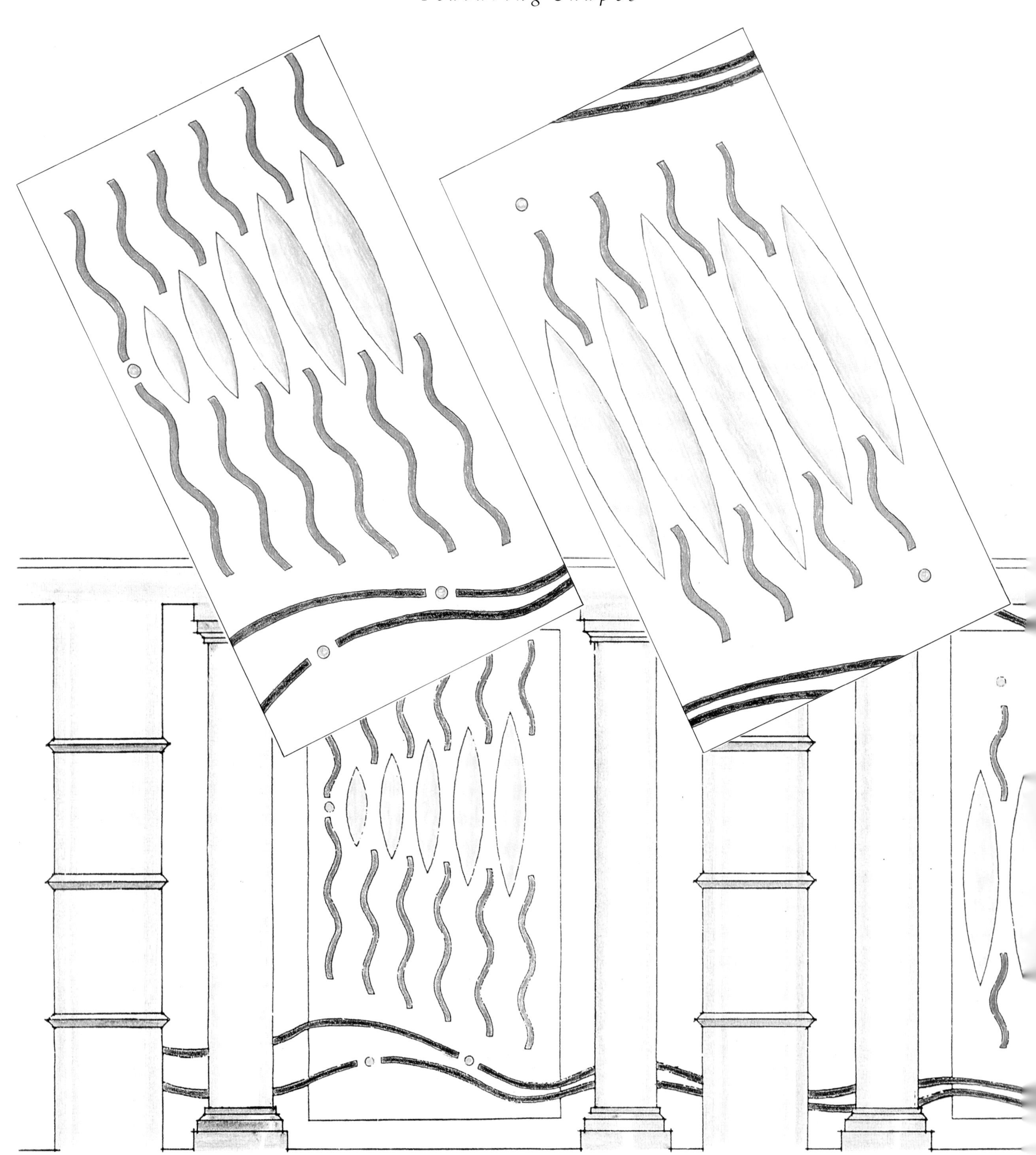

CARPETS

Featuring Shapes

Carpet does not have to be used only on the floor. In the past rugs were often used as wallhangings, both because of their value and to keep out draughts.

LEFT Colour is combined with texture to achieve a more complex three dimensional effect. This sample for a wallhanging rug shows cut and loop pile and different pile lengths, while outline carving gives definition to the design. The single deep carved line will frame the main area of the finished design.

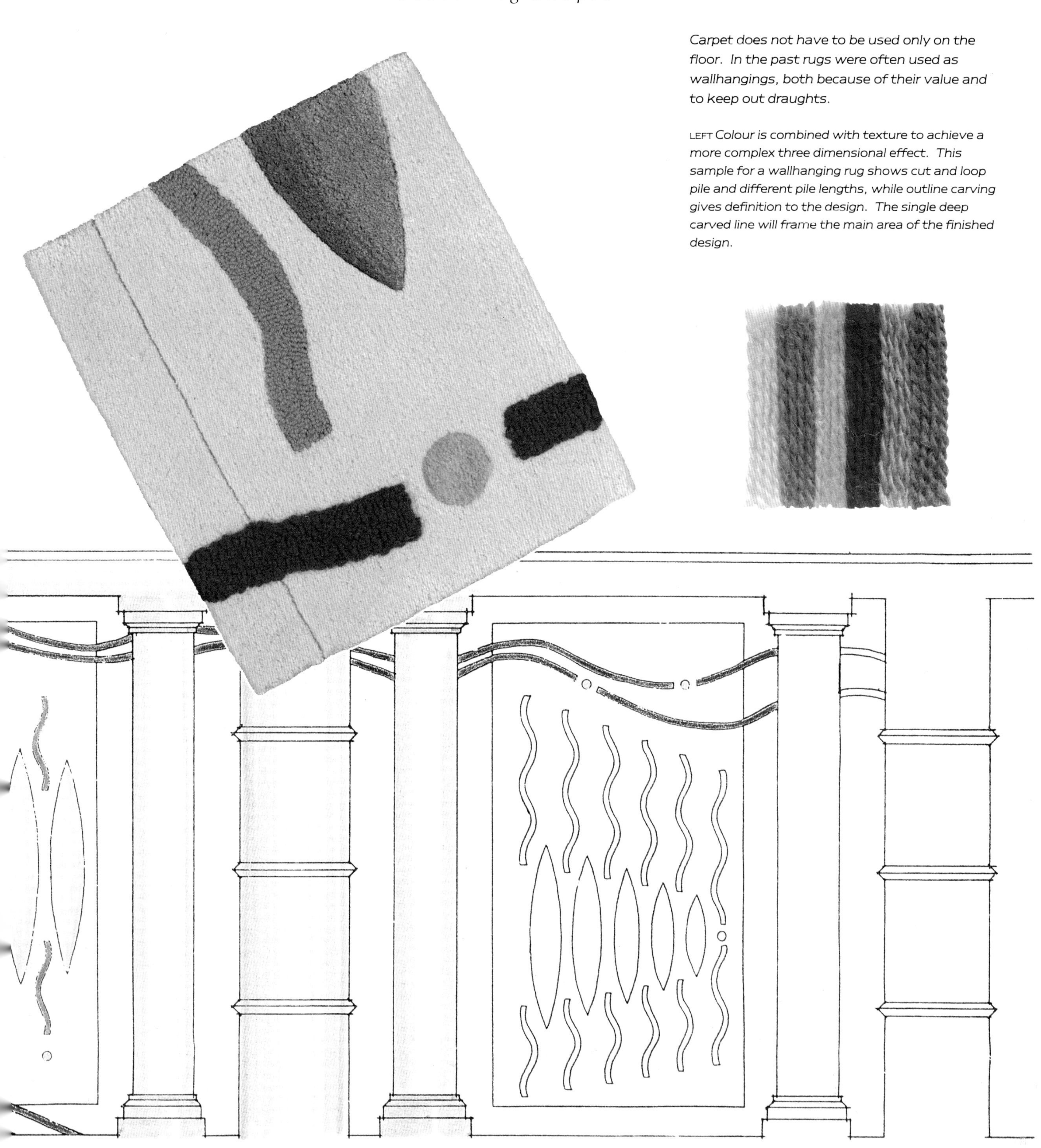

CARPETS
Setting a Style

LEFT *Complex border design using both geometric and flower motifs in seven colours. The central field is fully patterned.*

BELOW LEFT *Informal floral design in five colours with ribbon border.*

BELOW RIGHT *A more formal floral border in seven colours.*

CENTRE LEFT *Geometric border design in four colours with plain central field.*

CENTRE RIGHT *Simple geometric stylised leaf design in three colours, with carved geometric design to central field.*

BOTTOM LEFT *The geometric pattern of this carpet is softened by the use of flowing ribbons to make up the design.*

BOTTOM RIGHT *Combination of geometric and floral shapes in a border in seven colours, with a simple carved trellis set with flowers as the central field design.*

Machine made carpets do not have to have an all over repeat design. Here a machine made strip of patterned carpet is sewn into a plain background colour to make the central design feature.

The carpet in this dining room is also machine made, the border runs round each table in a series of rectangles. The carpet was woven in four metre strips, complete with borders, then assembled on site.

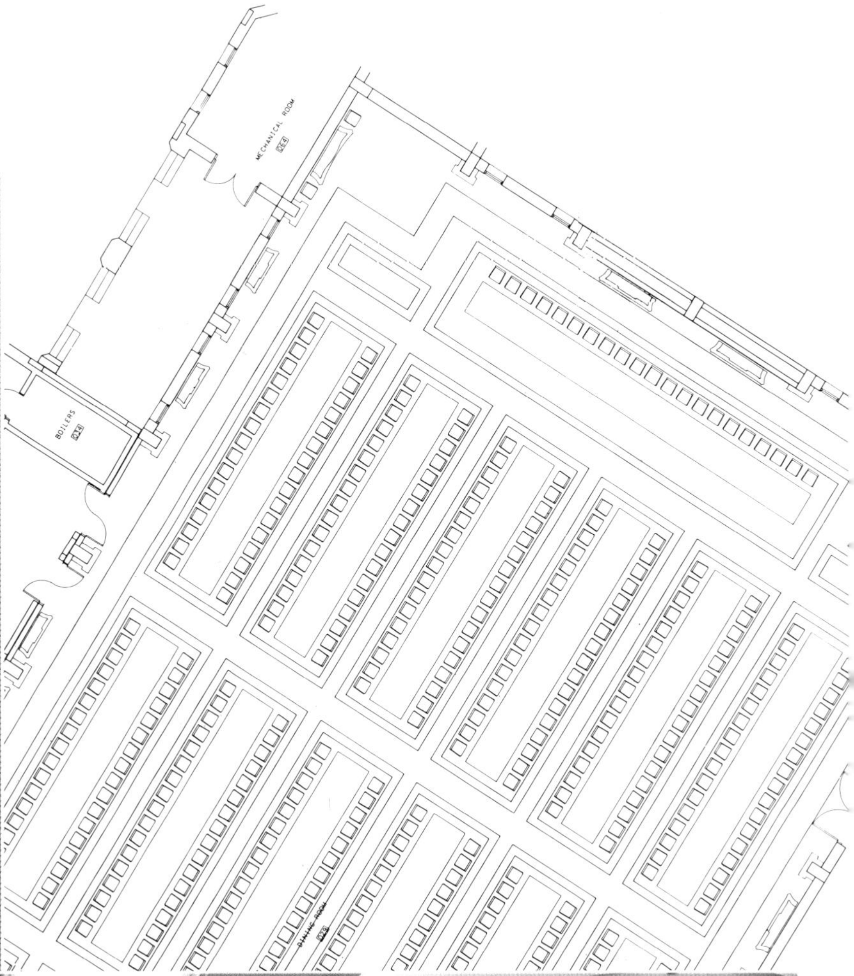

CARPETS
Understanding the Techniques

When designing a carpet it is important to start by working out where the borders and motifs will be placed in the room. This plan should be checked against the furniture layout to ensure nothing obscures major portions of the pattern, although the design should not follow the furniture layout too closely. A plain area should be left around the edge to allow the carpet to be cut round architectural features when it is laid.

The design itself is drawn up to scale and a section of the pattern coloured to indicate where each colour goes.

In the factory the design is scaled up to full size and transferred onto the backing cloth, which is usually cotton jute. Unless it is extremely large, the carpet is woven in one piece so there are no joins to cause problems when the carpet is installed. The backing cloth is stretched on the loom and the pile is tufted in by hand, one colour at a time, from the back. The wool is cut off automatically to the right length by the gun itself, there are different guns for cut or loop pile.

The carpet is removed from the loom and strong mesh is added and latexed Into place to make the carpet heavier and more stable. Any unevenness in the pile length is sheared off and the carpet is ready for final finishing. To add more definition to the design, the outline can be carved into the pile. Carving can also be used to add pattern to plain areas.

Carving means cutting a groove into the pile of a carpet after it has been woven. Fine line or hair line carving is often used to outline the colours in a multi colour design to accentuate the design. A very simple but effective technique is to carve a design into a plain colour carpet, thus achieving an interesting effect by texture only.

Embossing is done during the actual weaving of the carpet. Part of the design is woven with longer length pile, so that area of the carpet is at a higher level than the rest which produces a cameo style design.

Recessing is also done during the weaving, part of the design being woven with shorter length pile, producing an intaglio effect. Hard edges are often softened by rounding them off - this is known as beveling. All these techniques can be done on either plain or multi coloured carpets and with both cut or loop pile and can be also combined to give a very rich effect.

TOP Coloured artwork of the design has to be produced to work out repeats and identify the colour placement. The design may coordinate with another item in the room, such as curtains or upholstery.

ABOVE Matching the dyed wool to the original colour sample before weaving.

RIGHT Hand tufting the carpet on the loom.

OPPOSITE Carving lines with a hand held cutter into the surface of the finished carpet.

FURNITURE

Furniture can be selected to match or contrast with the overall style of the room and there is such a wide range of designs from different periods available that there should be no problem in finding something suitable for the most unusual interior scheme.

Original antique furniture is expensive and is not readily available, but many companies still make furniture to classical designs using the old manufacturing methods and doing much of the work by hand. Besides traditional finishes such as French polish, gold leaf or paint, they also use modern coatings so that the natural colour and grain of the wood can be highlighted and the furniture is easier to care for. The other advantage of these 'modern antiques' is that the interiors of cabinets and cupboards can be fitted out to take modern equipment such as stereos and televisions.

The techniques and finishes that were developed on period style furniture can also be used on more modern items. Dragged or mottled paintwork, lacquer or gold leaf can all look very stylish on contemporary design furniture, often adding a touch of richness and texture to simple shapes and forms.

OPPOSITE *Screen with imitation tortoiseshell finish done in gold and coloured lacquer, with matching console and side chair.*

BELOW *Desk in special mottled gold paint finish*

RIGHT Office with custom made oval desk in polished wood with gold leaf highlighting.

BELOW Details of the desk decoration are picked up in the wing chairs made for the same room.

BELOW RIGHT The desk is stained to match the wood panelling, the details are picked out in gold.

LEFT *A massive desk in a classically panelled office.*

BELOW *Original sketch design for the desk.*

BOTTOM *A desk nearly three metres long needs details that are large in scale. The dark stained wood and heavy use of gold leaf give the design an impressive solidity. The drawers are concealed behind doors for extra security.*

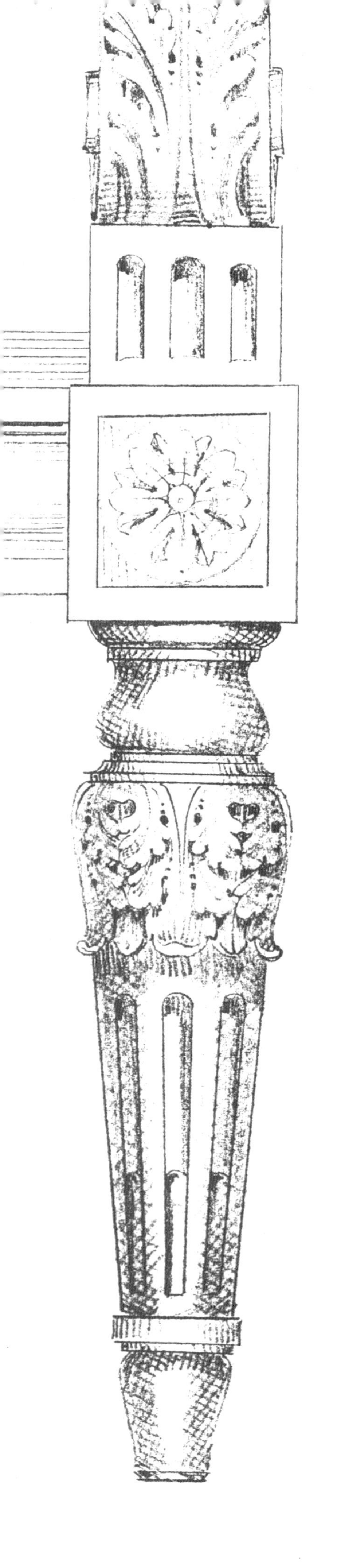

FURNITURE
Setting a Style

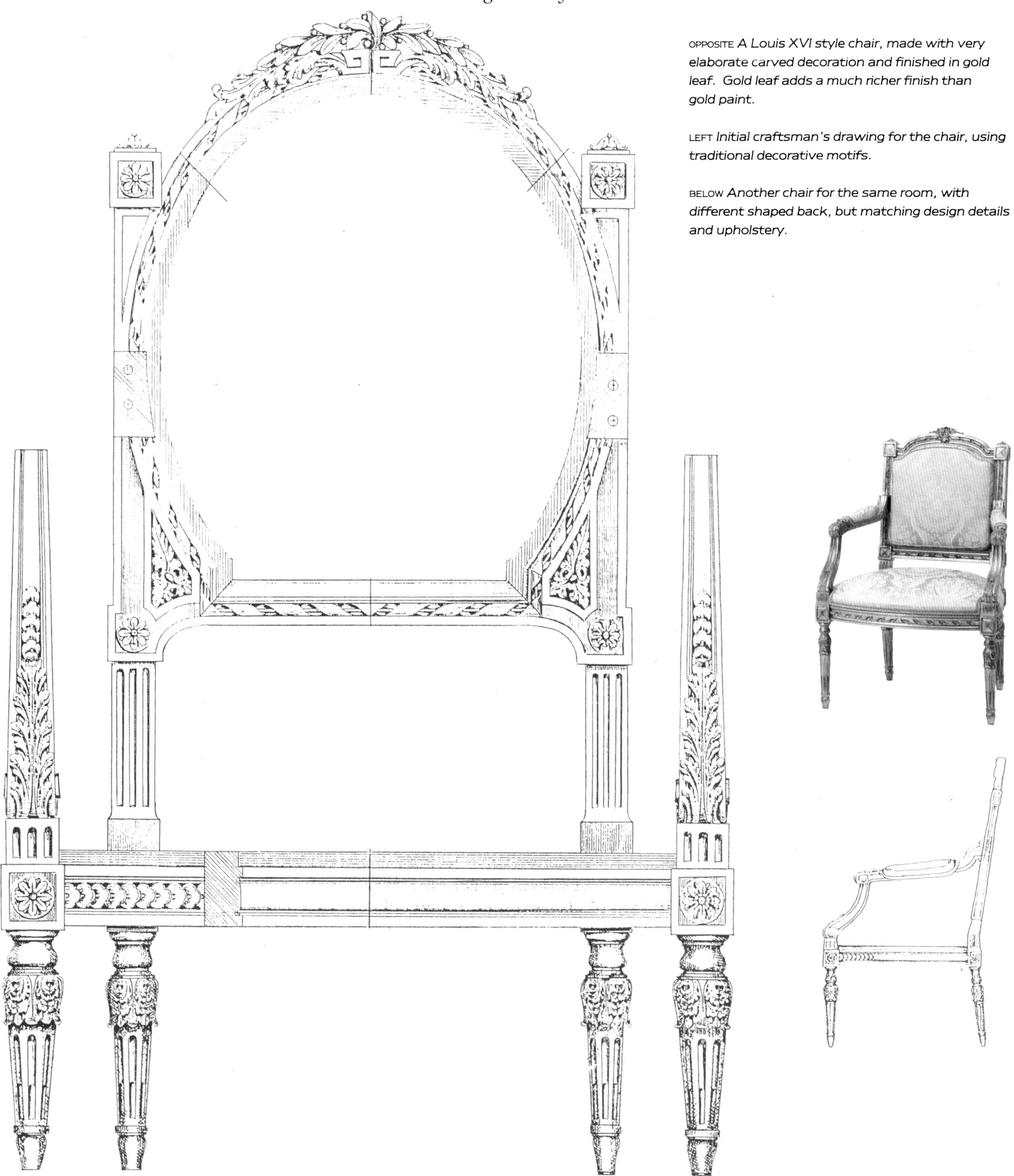

OPPOSITE *A Louis XVI style chair, made with very elaborate carved decoration and finished in gold leaf. Gold leaf adds a much richer finish than gold paint.*

LEFT *Initial craftsman's drawing for the chair, using traditional decorative motifs.*

BELOW *Another chair for the same room, with different shaped back, but matching design details and upholstery.*

FURNITURE

Attention to Details

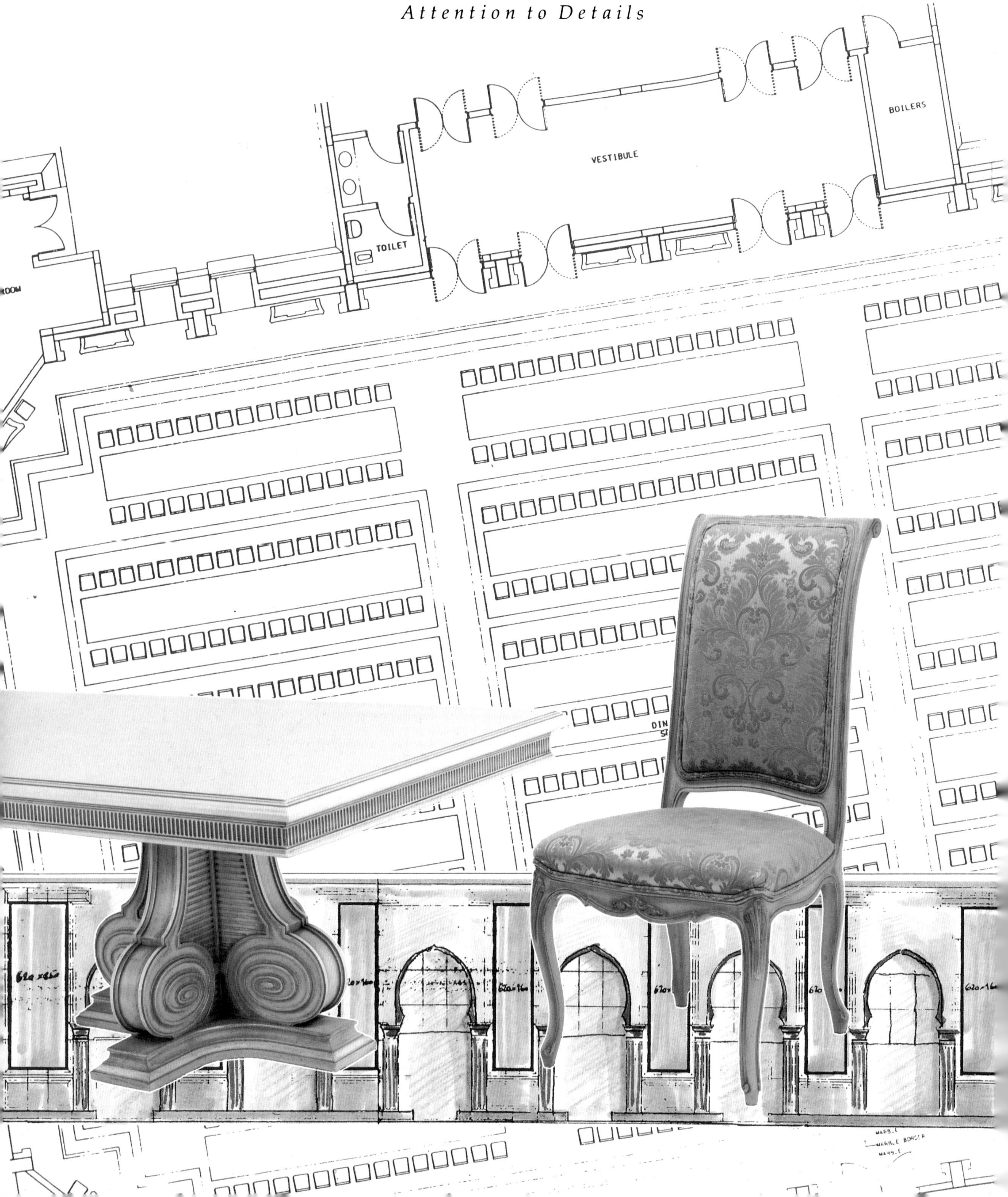

FURNITURE
Attention to Details

OPPOSITE *A simple and elegant dining chair with Louis XV style leg. The rolled detail from the back of the chair has been picked up in the base of the dining table.*

BELOW *The original perspective sketch.*

BOTTOM *The sideboards also pick up the same rolled detail. All the items have dragged paint finish with gold highlights.*

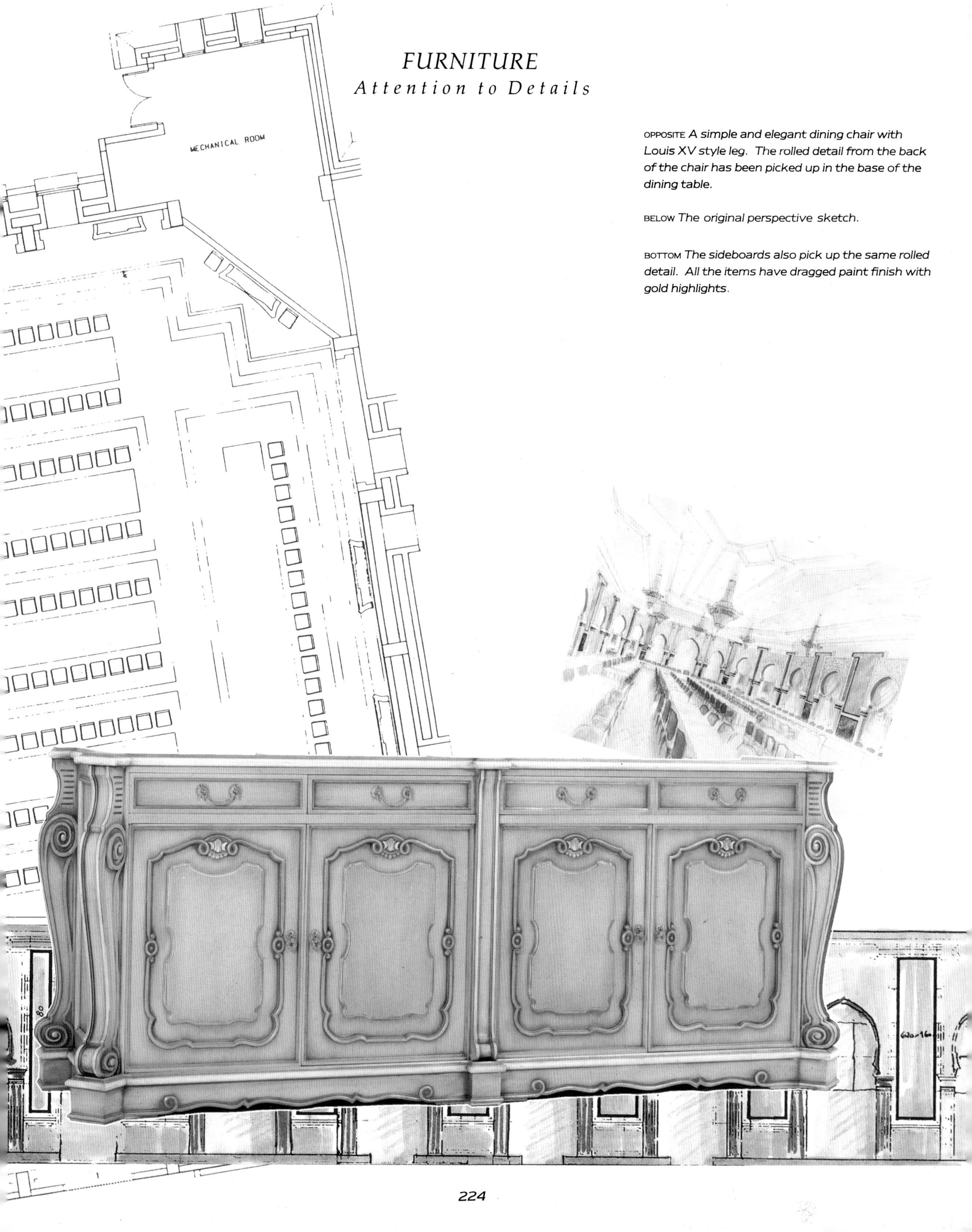

OPPOSITE *Chair and matching table in brightly coloured lacquer finish, for a swimming pool area. The colours for the lacquer are taken from the upholstery fabrics.*

LEFT *Small table for a dressing room, the top painted to match the carpet design. The cupboard doors also have the same ribbon and flowers motif, which was originally taken from one of the fabrics used in the room.*

FURNITURE
Using Pattern

OPPOSITE TOP *Dining table top inlaid in a complex design with coloured veneers. The picture below shows the table in situ.*

OPPOSITE BOTTOM LEFT *Table top with inlaid marble decoration.*

BELOW *Circular hall table with painted design.*

BOTTOM *Octagonal table top with inlaid wood design.*

OPPOSITE *Contemporary table base with three dimensional lattice design.*

OPPOSITE CENTRE LEFT *Elaborate leaf design base, highlighted in gold. The leaf motif is also picked up on the side of the table top.*

OPPOSITE BOTTOM LEFT *Table base designed to look like the capital of a column, with swags and other carved details picked out in gold leaf.*

CENTRE *Classic carved base with acanthus leaf motif for a circular table.*

BELOW LEFT *Simple four legged table base with urn shaped central pillar.*

BOTTOM LEFT *A composite style column capital also makes an ideal table base.*

BELOW *Two modern designs with simple coloured veneer decoration.*

OPPOSITE *Writing desk in French polished wood with flower design inlaid and painted. The detail of part of the design from the front of the desk shows the intricacy of the work.*

LEFT *Dressing table in polished satin wood, with painted decoration and gold coach lines, a copy of an antique piece dating from 1900. The mirror frame is hand carved.*

BELOW *Detail of some of the hand painted decoration.*

BELOW CENTRE *Furniture painted with landscape scenes was a typical 18th century decorative technique.*

BOTTOM *This bow fronted bedside cabinet is an exact copy of an antique original dating from 1755, painted in dark green with a patina finish and gold details. The landscape scene across the front and sides is hand painted.*

RIGHT *A television cabinet in the style of a vitrine, but with solid doors to hide the screen when it is not in use. Display storage and decorative features in the design hide its true purpose even more effectively. The door pulls down and slides away under the television when it is in use.*

LEFT *In this cabinet the shelf inside, on which the television stands, pulls out and swivels so that the screen can be viewed from all areas of the room. The cabinet is counterbalanced so that it does not overturn when the shelf is holding the television out to its fullest extent.*

BELOW *Another option is to do away with the doors altogether, and have the television rising up out of the top of the cabinet. The lifting mechanism can be wired to bring the television up automatically when it is switched on using the remote control. This solution is particularly useful if a low cabinet is needed to suit the room, as the cabinet does not have to be tall enough to hold the television at the correct viewing height.*

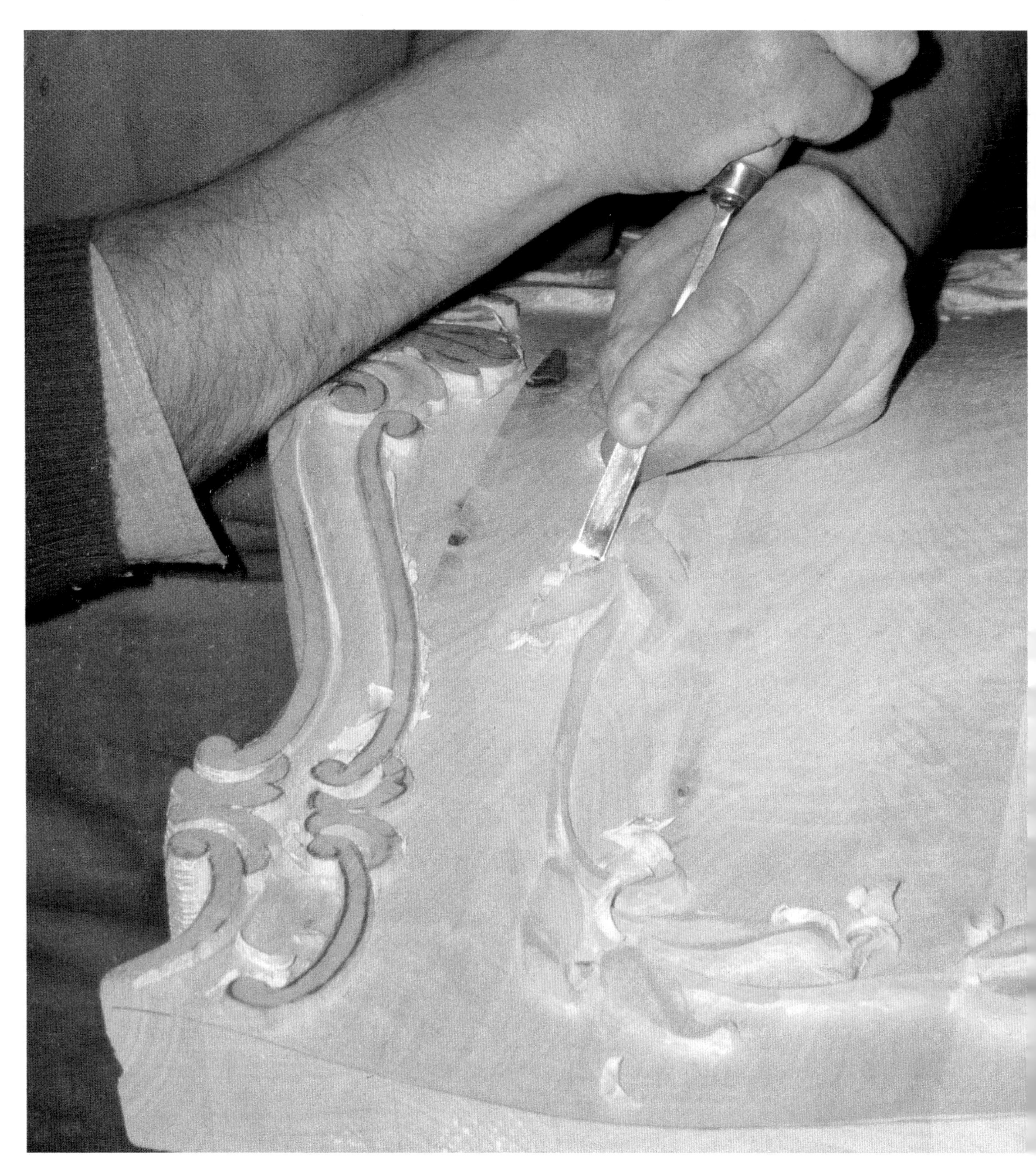

Wood used for fine furniture must be seasoned outside for several years before it can be used, or it will warp and split. Initial cutting is usually done by machine, but on the more expensive pieces the finishing or carving will be done by hand, using traditional methods and tools.

If the final item is to be painted then a less expensive plain wood, such as beech, can be used. If it is to be polished then a wood with an interesting grain, like walnut or sycamore may be selected. Of course the finished piece can be coloured and stained to look as if it is made of a different type of wood, just as some antique pieces were.

Traditional finishes such as French polishing are still used, but modern finishes can be easier to maintain. Decoration can be added by carving, or by inlaying different coloured veneers, or by applying paint.

OPPOSITE *The wood is shaped with a combination of machining by hand and hand carving.*

BELOW *Working out the details to be hand carved. The design will be drawn freehand directly onto the wood, then carved out.*

RIGHT *Adding painted decoration by hand.*

BOTTOM RIGHT *Before the gold leaf is applied by hand, the furniture is coated with a coloured base coat. The leaf is applied with a soft brush, then burnished in place.*

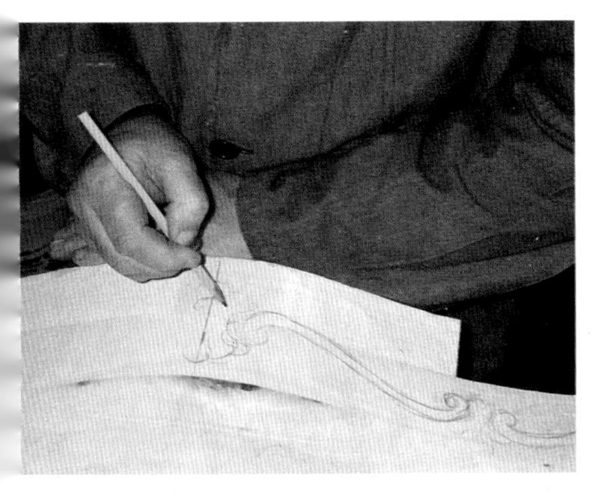

ACCESSORIES

Artwork and accessories add the final and most personal touch to an interior. They are as important as the colour scheme for creating the final ambiance of the room, making it formal or intimate, a place to work or a place to relax.

Artwork by its very nature is usually unique, a one off item made by a craftsman to his own design. Special pieces can quite easily be commissioned to add a touch of individuality to a room that might otherwise be similar to many others. It is important to remember that artwork should not be selected to match the colour scheme too closely or it will blend into the background and will not fulfill its function of making this statement of individuality.

Accessories can be functional as well as decorative - vases, bowls, linens, but despite this their decorative side should never be overlooked. The wrong shape or colour will instantly add a discordant note to the room and can ruin the effect that has been so carefully built up with the rest of the design.

OPPOSITE *Accessories add an individual touch to a room and can be collected from many countries. Here a model house from America, a glass pot from Italy, an English painting and a French tapestry and china all coordinate together.*

BELOW *Decorative bowls and plates from China add a splash of colour.*

RIGHT *A collection of accessories for a room in a country house. The tapestry with its decorative birds suggested the addition of a wood and wicker birdcage to the room.*

BELOW *The colours in the tapestry are picked up in the pots and vases.*

LEFT AND BELOW *Decorative urns on stands are useful to add interest to odd corners. Sketch designs for a two foot high bronze urn with a patina finish, standing on a marble base.*

BOTTOM LEFT *Patina being applied to the bronze urn.*

OPPOSITE *This bronze pot with green enamel finish is over six feet high on its brass stand. Eighteen of them were made and used to line the sides of a massive formal entrance hall.*

FAR RIGHT *Full scale mock up design of the pot in coloured plaster.*

BELOW *Screens were originally used to keep out draughts and were normally positioned in front of doors. Now their function is usually merely decorative. This screen in stretched and painted fabric has been decorated using motifs from the carpet design.*

OPPOSITE *A painted wood screen in three sections, the design based on a wrought iron gate.*

OPPOSITE BOTTOM *Detail of the painted design.*

LEFT *Table lamps not only add extra light, but are useful decorative features. Here the classical style of the lamp matches the style of the room.*

BOTTOM LEFT *Matching gold framed mirrors pick up the gold detailing in the panelling. The elaborate antique gold clock adds a further touch of richness.*

BELOW *A symmetrical layout can be very effective. The brass lamps add a warm gleam to the room and the cushions on the sofa pick up some of the colours in the picture above.*

BOTTOM *Pictures that are hung on panelled walls should relate in size and shape to the panel.*

OPPOSITE *Mirrors add an extra dimension to a room, creating a feeling of spaciousness and light.*

RIGHT *Monogrammed tableware and linens add a personal touch to a table setting.*

BELOW *The china, cutlery, glass & linen used in this scheme, showing how the monogram has been incorporated on each item.*

OPPOSITE *Here the glasses and china coordinate with the same design in gold, so the linen for the table has been selected with gold embroidery to match.*

OPPOSITE *Set of matching bathroom accessories in white towelling with yellow embroidery. The embroidered motif can pick up a colour or a theme from the rest of the room.*

LEFT *Table linen can be decorated with an embroidered motif. Many standard designs are available, but it is also relatively easy to have special designs created without vast expense.*

BOTTOM LEFT *Linen pillowcases with embroidered decoration.*